D1240983

International Law
Chiefly as Interpreted and Applied in Canada

Documentary Supplement

HUGH M. KINDRED and PHILLIP M. SAUNDERS
General Editors
Faculty of Law
Dalhousie University

JUTTA BRUNNÉE
Faculty of Law
University of Toronto

ROBERT J. CURRIE
Faculty of Law
Dalhousie University

TED L. McDORMAN
Faculty of Law
University of Victoria

ARMAND L.C. de MESTRAL
Faculty of Law
McGill University

KARIN MICKELSON
Faculty of Law
University of British Columbia

RENÉ PROVOST
Faculty of Law
McGill University

LINDA C. REIF
Faculty of Law
University of Alberta

STEPHEN J. TOOPE
Faculty of Law
McGill University

SHARON A. WILLIAMS
Osgoode Hall Law School
York University

SEVENTH EDITION
2006
EMOND MONTGOMERY PUBLICATIONS LIMITED

Emond Montgomery Publications Limited
60 Shaftesbury Avenue
Toronto ON M4T 1A3
http://www.emp.ca

Printed in Canada.

Edited, designed, and typeset by WordsWorth Communications, Toronto.

We acknowledge the financial support of the Government of Canada through the Book Publishing Industry Development Program (BPIDP) for our publishing activities.

Library and Archives Canada Cataloguing in Publication

International law, chiefly as interpreted and applied in Canada, seventh edition. Documentary supplement / Hugh M. Kindred and Phillip M. Saunders, general editors ; Jutta Brunee ... [et al.].

ISBN 1-55239-164-7

1. International law—Sources.   I. Kindred, Hugh M.   II. Saunders, Phillip Martin

KZ358.A2I57 2006 Suppl.   341′.0971   C2005-907294-6

Preface

This set of documents is a supplement to the Seventh Edition of *International Law Chiefly as Interpreted and Applied in Canada*. It contains many of the major instruments of international law. When read together with the extracts of other legal sources reproduced in the book itself, they make up a compilation of basic materials on international law. It is hoped that this format of placing the major and recurring international legal texts in a separate supplement will provide an easy means of referral for readers. In the interest of keeping the supplement within a convenient size, not all the documents are reproduced in their entirety—for example, insubstantial provisions such as the final clauses of conventions have been omitted. However, the whole of every legal source reproduced in this supplement or extracted in the book itself may be readily accessed through the supporting website located at <http://www.emp.ca/intlaw7>.

November 2005   Hugh M. Kindred & Phillip M. Saunders
                                                              General Editors

Table of Contents

I
Charter of the United Nations

As Signed 1945 and Amended 1965, 1968 and 1973

WE THE PEOPLES OF THE UNITED NATIONS DETERMINED to save succeeding generations from the scourge of war, which twice in our life-time has brought untold sorrow to mankind, and

to reaffirm faith in fundamental human rights, in the dignity and worth of the human person, in the equal rights of men and women and of nations large and small, and

to establish conditions under which justice and respect for the obligations arising from treaties and other sources of international law can be maintained, and

to promote social progress and better standards of life in larger freedom,

AND FOR THESE ENDS to practice tolerance and live together in peace with one another as good neighbours, and

to unite our strength to maintain international peace and security, and

to ensure, by the acceptance of principles and the institution of methods, that armed force shall not be used, save in the common interest, and

to employ international machinery for the promotion of the economic and social advancement of all peoples,

HAVE RESOLVED TO COMBINE OUR EFFORTS TO ACCOMPLISH THESE AIMS
Accordingly, our respective Governments, through representatives assembled in the city of San Francisco, who have exhibited their full powers found to be in good and due form, have agreed to the present Charter of the United Nations and do hereby establish an international organization to be known as the United Nations.

CHAPTER I
PURPOSES AND PRINCIPLES

Article 1

The Purposes of the United Nations are:

1. To maintain international peace and security, and to that end: to take effective collective measures for the prevention and removal of threats to the peace, and for the suppression of acts of aggression or other breaches of the peace, and to bring about by peaceful means, and in conformity with the principles of justice and international law, adjustment or settlement of international disputes or situations which lead to a breach of the peace;

2. To develop friendly relations among nations based on respect for the principle of equal rights and self-determination of peoples, and to take other appropriate measures to strengthen universal peace;

3. To achieve international co-operation in solving international problems of an economic, social, cultural, or humanitarian character, and in promoting and encouraging respect for human rights and for fundamental freedoms for all without distinction as to race, sex, language, or religion; and

4. To be a centre for harmonizing the actions of nations in the attainment of these common ends.

Article 2

The Organization and its Members, in pursuit of the Purposes stated in Article 1, shall act in accordance with the following Principles.

1. The Organization is based on the principle of the sovereign equality of all its Members.

2. All Members, in order to ensure to all of them the rights and benefits resulting from membership, shall fulfil in good faith the obligations assumed by them in accordance with the present Charter.

3. All Members shall settle their international disputes by peaceful means in such a manner that international peace and security, and justice, are not endangered.

4. All Members shall refrain in their international relations from the threat or use of force against the territorial integrity or political independence of any state, or in any other manner inconsistent with the Purposes of the United Nations.

5. All Members shall give the United Nations every assistance in any action it takes in accordance with the present Charter, and shall refrain from giving assistance to any state against which the United Nations is taking preventive or enforcement action.

6. The Organization shall ensure that states which are not Members of the United Nations act in accordance with these Principles so far as may be necessary for the maintenance of international peace and security.

7. Nothing contained in the present Charter shall authorize the United Nations to intervene in matters which are essentially within the domestic jurisdiction of any state or shall require the Members to submit such matters to settlement under the present Charter; but this principle shall not prejudice the application of enforcement measures under Chapter VII.

CHAPTER II
MEMBERSHIP

Article 3

The original Members of the United Nations shall be the states which, having participated in the United Nations Conference on International Organization at San Francisco, or having previously signed the Declaration by United Nations of 1 January 1942, sign the present Charter and ratify it in accordance with Article 110.

Article 4

1. Membership in the United Nations is open to all other peace-loving states which accept the obligations contained in the present Charter and, in the judgment of the Organization, are able and willing to carry out these obligations.

2. The admission of any such state to membership in the United Nations will be effected by a decision of the General Assembly upon the recommendation of the Security Council.

Article 5

A Member of the United Nations against which preventive or enforcement action has been taken by the Security Council may be suspended from the exercise of the rights and privileges of membership by the General Assembly upon the recommendation of the Security Council. The exercise of these rights and privileges may be restored by the Security Council.

Article 6
A Member of the United Nations which has persistently violated the Principles contained in the present Charter may be expelled from the Organization by the General Assembly upon the recommendation of the Security Council.

CHAPTER III
ORGANS

Article 7
1. There are established as the principal organs of the United Nations: a General Assembly, a Security Council, an Economic and Social Council, a Trusteeship Council, an International Court of Justice, and a Secretariat.

2. Such subsidiary organs as may be found necessary may be established in accordance with the present Charter.

Article 8
The United Nations shall place no restrictions on the eligibility of men and women to participate in any capacity and under conditions of equality in its principal and subsidiary organs.

CHAPTER IV
THE GENERAL ASSEMBLY

Composition

Article 9
1. The General Assembly shall consist of all the Members of the United Nations.
2. Each Member shall have not more than five representatives in the General Assembly.

Functions and powers

Article 10
The General Assembly may discuss any questions or any matters within the scope of the present Charter or relating to the powers and functions of any organs provided for in the present Charter, and, except as provided in Article 12, may make recommendations to the Members of the United Nations or to the Security Council or to both on any such questions or matters.

Article 11
1. The General Assembly may consider the general principles of co-operation in the maintenance of international peace and security, including the principles governing disarmament and the regulation of armaments, and may make recommendations with regard to such principles to the Members or to the Security Council or to both.

2. The General Assembly may discuss any questions relating to the maintenance of international peace and security brought before it by any Member of the United Nations, or by the Security Council, or by a state which is not a Member of the United Nations in accordance with Article 35, paragraph 2, and, except as provided in Article 12, may make recommendations with regard to any such questions to the state or states concerned or to the Security Council or to both. Any such question on which action is necessary shall be referred to the Security Council by the General Assembly either before or after discussion.

3. The General Assembly may call the attention of the Security Council to situations which are likely to endanger international peace and security.

4. The powers of the General Assembly set forth in this Article shall not limit the general scope of Article 10.

Article 12

1. While the Security Council is exercising in respect of any dispute or situation the functions assigned to it in the present Charter, the General Assembly shall not make any recommendation with regard to that dispute or situation unless the Security Council so requests.

2. The Secretary-General, with the consent of the Security Council, shall notify the General Assembly at each session of any matters relative to the maintenance of international peace and security which are being dealt with by the Security Council and shall similarly notify the General Assembly, or the Members of the United Nations if the General Assembly is not in session, immediately the Security Council ceases to deal with such matters.

Article 13

1. The General Assembly shall initiate studies and make recommendations for the purpose of:

(a) promoting international co-operation in the political field and encouraging the progressive development of international law and its codification;

(b) promoting international co-operation in the economic, social, cultural, educational, and health fields, and assisting in the realization of human rights and fundamental freedoms for all without distinction as to race, sex, language or religion.

2. The further responsibilities, functions and powers of the General Assembly with respect to matters mentioned in paragraph (1)(b) above are set forth in Chapters IX and X.

Article 14

Subject to the provisions of Article 12, the General Assembly may recommend measures for the peaceful adjustment of any situation, regardless of origin, which it deems likely to impair the general welfare or friendly relations among nations, including situations resulting from a violation of the provisions of the present Charter setting forth the Purposes and Principles of the United Nations.

Article 15

1. The General Assembly shall receive and consider annual and special reports from the Security Council; these reports shall include an account of the measures that the Security Council has decided upon or taken to maintain international peace and security.

2. The General Assembly shall receive and consider reports from the other organs of the United Nations.

Article 16

The General Assembly shall perform such functions with respect to the international trusteeship system as are assigned to it under Chapters XII and XIII, including the approval of the trusteeship agreements for areas not designated as strategic.

Article 17

1. The General Assembly shall consider and approve the budget of the Organization.

2. The expenses of the Organization shall be borne by the Members as apportioned by the General Assembly.

3. The General Assembly shall consider and approve any financial and budgetary arrangements with specialized agencies referred to in Article 57 and shall examine the administrative budgets of such specialized agencies with a view to making recommendations to the agencies concerned.

Voting

Article 18

1. Each member of the General Assembly shall have one vote.

2. Decisions of the General Assembly on important questions shall be made by two thirds majority of the members present and voting. These questions shall include: recommendations with respect to the maintenance of international peace and security, the election of the non-permanent members of the Security Council, the election of the members of the Economic and Social Council, the election of members of the Trusteeship Council in accordance with paragraph 1(c) of Article 86, the admission of new Members to the United Nations, the suspension of the rights and privileges of membership, the expulsion of Members, questions relating to the operation of the trusteeship system, and budgetary questions.

3. Decisions on other questions, including the determination of additional categories of questions to be decided by a two-thirds majority, shall be made by a majority of the members present and voting.

Article 19

A Member of the United Nations which is in arrears in the payment of its financial contributions to the Organization shall have no vote in the General Assembly if the amount of its arrears equals or exceeds the amount of the contributions due from it for the preceding two full years. The General Assembly may, nevertheless, permit such a Member to vote if it is satisfied that the failure to pay is due to conditions beyond the control of the Member.

Procedure

Article 20

The General Assembly shall meet in regular annual sessions and in such special sessions as occasion may require. Special sessions shall be convoked by the Secretary-General at the request of the Security Council or of a majority of the Members of the United Nations.

Article 21

The General Assembly shall adopt its own rules of procedure. It shall elect its President for each session.

Article 22

The General Assembly may establish such subsidiary organs as it deems necessary for the performance of its functions.

CHAPTER V
THE SECURITY COUNCIL

Composition

Article 23

1. The Security Council shall consist of fifteen Members of the United Nations. The Republic of China, France, the Union of Soviet Socialist Republics, the United Kingdom of Great Britain and Northern Ireland, and the United States of America shall be permanent members of the Security Council. The General Assembly shall elect ten other Members of the United Nations to be non-permanent members of the Security Council, due regard being specially paid, in the first instance to the contribution of Members of the United Nations to the maintenance of international peace and security and to the other purposes of the Organization, and also to equitable geographical distribution.

2. The non-permanent members of the Security Council shall be elected for a term of two years. In the first election of the non-permanent members after the increase of the membership of the Security Council from eleven to fifteen, two of the four additional members shall be chosen for a term of one year. A retiring member shall not be eligible for immediate re-election.

3. Each member of the Security Council shall have one representative.

Functions and Powers

Article 24

1. In order to ensure prompt and effective action by the United Nations, its Members confer on the Security Council primary responsibility for the maintenance of international peace and security, and agree that in carrying out its duties under this responsibility the Security Council acts on their behalf.

2. In discharging these duties the Security Council shall act in accordance with the Purposes and Principles of the United Nations. The specific powers granted to the Security Council for the discharge of these duties are laid down in Chapters VI, VII, VIII, and XII.

3. The Security Council shall submit annual and, when necessary, special reports to the General Assembly for its consideration.

Article 25

The Members of the United Nations agree to accept and carry out the decisions of the Security Council in accordance with the present Charter.

Article 26

In order to promote the establishment and maintenance of international peace and security with the least diversion for armaments of the world's human and economic resources, the Security Council shall be responsible for formulating, with the assistance of the Military Staff Committee referred to in Article 47, plans to be submitted to the Members of the United Nations for the establishment of a system for the regulation of armaments.

Voting

Article 27

1. Each member of the Security Council shall have one vote.

2. Decisions of the Security Council on procedural matters shall be made by an affirmative vote of nine members.

3. Decisions of the Security Council on all other matters shall be made by an affirmative vote of nine members including the concurring votes of the permanent members; provided that, in decisions under Chapter VI, and under paragraph 3 of Article 52, a party to a dispute shall abstain from voting.

Procedure

Article 28

1. The Security Council shall be so organized as to be able to function continuously. Each member of the Security Council shall for this purpose be represented at all times at the seat of the Organization.

2. The Security Council shall hold periodic meetings at which each of it members may, if it so desires, be represented by a member of the government or by some other specially designated representative.

3. The Security Council may hold meetings at such places other than the seat of the Organization as in its judgment will best facilitate its work.

Article 29

The Security Council may establish such subsidiary organs as it deems necessary for the performance of its functions.

Article 30

The Security Council shall adopt its own rules of procedure, including the method of selecting its President.

Article 31

Any Member of the United Nations which is not a member of the Security Council may participate, without vote, in the discussion of any question brought before the Security Council whenever the latter considers that the interests of that Member are specially affected.

Article 32

Any Member of the United Nations which is not a member of the Security Council or any state which is not a Member of the United Nations, if it is a party to a dispute under consideration by the Security Council, shall be invited to participate, without vote, in the discussion relating to the dispute. The Security Council shall lay down such conditions as it deems just for the participation of a state which is not a Member of the United Nations.

CHAPTER VI
PACIFIC SETTLEMENT OF DISPUTES

Article 33

1. The parties to any dispute, the continuance of which is likely to endanger the maintenance of international peace and security, shall, first of all, seek a solution by negotiation, enquiry, mediation, conciliation, arbitration, judicial settlement, resort to regional agencies or arrangements, or other peaceful means of their own choice.

2. The Security Council shall, when it deems necessary, call upon the parties to settle their dispute by such means.

Article 34

The Security Council may investigate any dispute, or any situation which might lead to international friction or give rise to a dispute, in order to determine whether the continuance of the dispute or situation is likely to endanger the maintenance of international peace and security.

Article 35

1. Any Member of the United Nations may bring any dispute, or any situation of the nature referred to in Article 34, to the attention of the Security Council or of the General Assembly.

2. A state which is not a Member of the United Nations may bring to the attention of the Security Council or of the General Assembly any dispute to which it is a party if it accepts in advance, for the purposes of the dispute, the obligations of pacific settlement provided in the present Charter.

3. The proceedings of the General Assembly in respect of matters brought to its attention under this Article will be subject to the provisions of Articles 11 and 12.

Article 36

1. The Security Council may, at any stage of a dispute of the nature referred to in Article 33 or of a situation of like nature, recommend appropriate procedures or methods of adjustment.

2. The Security Council should take into consideration any procedures for the settlement of the dispute which have already been adopted by the parties.

3. In making recommendations under this Article the Security Council should also take into consideration that legal disputes should as a general rule be referred by the parties to the International Court of Justice in accordance with the provisions of the Statute of the Court.

Article 37

1. Should the parties to a dispute of the nature referred to in Article 33 fail to settle it by the means indicated in that Article, they shall refer it to the Security Council.

2. If the Security Council deems that the continuance of the dispute is in fact likely to

endanger the maintenance of international peace and security, it shall decide whether to take action under Article 36 or to recommend such terms of settlement as it may consider appropriate.

Article 38

Without prejudice to the provisions of Articles 33 to 37, the Security Council may, if all the parties to any dispute so request, make recommendations to the parties with a view to a pacific settlement of the dispute.

CHAPTER VII
ACTION WITH RESPECT TO THREATS TO THE PEACE, BREACHES OF THE PEACE, AND ACTS OF AGGRESSION

Article 39

The Security Council shall determine the existence of any threat to the peace, breach of the peace, or act of aggression and shall make recommendations, or decide what measures shall be taken in accordance with Articles 41 and 42, to maintain or restore international peace and security.

Article 40

In order to prevent an aggravation of the situation, the Security Council may, before making the recommendations or deciding upon the measures provided for in Article 39, call upon the parties concerned to comply with such provisional measures as it deems necessary or desirable. Such provisional measures shall be without prejudice to the rights, claims, or position of the parties concerned. The Security Council shall duly take account of failure to comply with such provisional measures.

Article 41

The Security Council may decide what measures not involving the use of armed force are to be employed to give effect to its decisions, and it may call upon the Members of the United Nations to apply such measures. These may include complete or partial interruption of economic relations and of rail, sea, air, postal, telegraphic, radio, and other means of communication, and the severance of diplomatic relations.

Article 42

Should the Security Council consider that measures provided for in Article 41 would be inadequate or have proved to be inadequate, it may take such action by air, sea, or land forces as may be necessary to maintain or restore international peace and security. Such action may include demonstrations, blockade, and other operations by air, sea, or land forces of Members of the United Nations.

Article 43

1. All Members of the United Nations, in order to contribute to the maintenance of international peace and security, undertake to make available to the Security Council, on its

call and in accordance with a special agreement or agreements, armed forces, assistance, and facilities, including rights of passage, necessary for the purpose of maintaining international peace and security.

2. Such agreement or agreements shall govern the numbers and types of forces, their degree of readiness and general location, and the nature of the facilities and assistance to be provided.

3. The agreement or agreements shall be negotiated as soon as possible on the initiative of the Security Council. They shall be concluded between the Security Council and Members or between the Security Council and groups of Members and shall be subject to ratification by the signatory states in accordance with their respective constitutional processes.

Article 44

When the Security Council has decided to use force it shall, before calling upon a Member not represented on it to provide armed forces in fulfilment of the obligations assumed under Article 43, invite that Member, if the Member so desires, to participate in the decisions of the Security Council concerning the employment of contingents of that Member's armed forces.

Article 45

In order to enable the United Nations to take urgent military measures, Members shall hold immediately available national air-force contingents for combined international enforcement action. The strength and degree of readiness of these contingents and plans for their combined action shall be determined, within the limits laid down in the special agreement or agreements referred to in Article 43, by the Security Council with the assistance of the Military Staff Committee.

Article 46

Plans for the application of armed force shall be made by the Security Council with the assistance of the Military Staff Committee.

Article 47

1. There shall be established a Military Staff Committee to advise and assist the Security Council on all questions relating to the Security Council's military requirements for the maintenance of international peace and security, the employment and command of forces placed at its disposal, the regulation of armaments, and possible disarmament.

2. The Military Staff Committee shall consist of the Chiefs of Staff of the permanent members of the Security Council or their representatives. Any Member of the United Nations not permanently represented on the Committee shall be invited by the Committee to be associated with it when the efficient discharge of the Committee's responsibilities requires the participation of that Member in its work.

3. The Military Staff Committee shall be responsible under the Security Council for the strategic direction of any armed forces placed at the disposal of the Security Council. Questions relating to the command of such forces shall be worked out subsequently.

4. The Military Staff Committee, with the authorization of the Security Council and after consultation with appropriate regional agencies, may establish regional subcommittees.

Article 48

1. The action required to carry out the decisions of the Security Council for the maintenance of international peace and security shall be taken by all the Members of the United Nations or by some of them, as the Security Council may determine.

2. Such decisions shall be carried out by the Members of the United Nations directly and through their action in the appropriate international agencies of which they are members.

Article 49

The Members of the United Nations shall join in affording mutual assistance in carrying out the measures decided upon by the Security Council.

Article 50

If preventive or enforcement measures against any state are taken by the Security Council, any other state, whether a Member of the United Nations or not, which finds itself confronted with special economic problems arising from the carrying out of those measures shall have the right to consult the Security Council with regard to a solution of those problems.

Article 51

Nothing in the present Charter shall impair the inherent right of individual or collective self-defence if an armed attack occurs against a Member of the United Nations, until the Security Council has taken measures necessary to maintain international peace and security. Measures taken by Members in the exercise of this right of self-defence shall be immediately reported to the Security Council and shall not in any way affect the authority and responsibility of the Security Council under the present Charter to take at any time such action as it deems necessary in order to maintain or restore international peace and security.

CHAPTER VIII
REGIONAL ARRANGEMENTS

Article 52

1. Nothing in the present Charter precludes the existence of regional arrangements or agencies for dealing with such matters relating to the maintenance of international peace and security as are appropriate for regional action, provided that such arrangements or agencies and their activities are consistent with the Purposes and Principles of the United Nations.

2. The Members of the United Nations entering into such arrangements or constituting such agencies shall make every effort to achieve pacific settlement of local disputes through such regional arrangements or by such regional agencies before referring them to the Security Council.

3. The Security Council shall encourage the development of pacific settlement of local disputes through such regional arrangements or by such regional agencies either on the initiative of the states concerned or by reference from the Security Council.

4. This Article in no way impairs the application of Articles 34 and 35.

Article 53

1. The Security Council shall, where appropriate, utilize such regional arrangements or agencies for enforcement action under its authority. But no enforcement action shall be taken under regional arrangements or by regional agencies without the authorization of the Security Council, with the exception of measures against any enemy state, as defined in paragraph 2 of this Article, provided for pursuant to Article 107 or in regional arrangements directed against renewal of aggressive policy on the part of any such state, until such time as the Organization may, on request of the Governments concerned, be charged with the responsibility for preventing further aggression by such a state.

2. The term enemy state as used in paragraph 1 of this Article applies to any state which during the Second World War has been an enemy of any signatory of the present Charter.

Article 54

The Security Council shall at all times be kept fully informed of activities undertaken or in contemplation under regional arrangements or by regional agencies for the maintenance of international peace and security.

CHAPTER IX
INTERNATIONAL ECONOMIC AND SOCIAL CO-OPERATION

Article 55

With a view to the creation of conditions of stability and well-being which are necessary for peaceful and friendly relations among nations based on respect for the principle of equal rights and self-determination of peoples, the United Nations shall promote:

(a) higher standards of living, full employment, and conditions of economic and social progress and development;

(b) solutions of international economic, social, health, and related problems; and international cultural and educational co-operation; and

(c) universal respect for, and observance of, human rights and fundamental freedoms for all without distinction as to race, sex, language, or religion.

Article 56

All Members pledge themselves to take joint and separate action in co-operation with the Organization for the achievement of the purposes set forth in Article 55.

Article 57

1. The various specialized agencies, established by intergovernmental agreement and having wide international responsibilities, as defined in their basic instruments, in economic, social, cultural, health, and related fields, shall be brought into relationship with the United Nations in accordance with the provisions of Article 63.

2. Such agencies thus brought into relationship with the United Nations are hereinafter referred to as specialized agencies.

Article 58

The Organization shall make recommendations for the co-ordination of the policies and activities of the specialized agencies.

Article 59

The Organization shall, where appropriate, initiate negotiations among the states concerned for the creation of any new specialized agencies required for the accomplishment of the purposes set forth in Article 55.

Article 60

Responsibility for the discharge of the functions of the Organization set forth in this Chapter shall be vested in the General Assembly and, under the authority of the General Assembly, in the Economic and Social Council, which shall have for this purpose the powers set forth in Chapter X.

CHAPTER X
THE ECONOMIC AND SOCIAL COUNCIL

Composition

Article 61

1. The Economic and Social Council shall consist of fifty-four Members of the United Nations elected by the General Assembly.

2. Subject to the provisions of paragraph 3, eighteen members of the Economic and Social Council shall be elected each year for a term of three years. A retiring member shall be eligible for immediate re-election.

3. At the first election after the increase in the membership of the Economic and Social Council from twenty-seven to fifty-four members, in addition to the members elected in place of the nine members whose term of office expires at the end of that year, twenty-seven additional members shall be elected. Of these twenty-seven additional members, the term of office of nine members so elected shall expire at the end of one year, and of nine other members at the end of two years, in accordance with arrangements made by the General Assembly.

4. Each member of the Economic and Social Council shall have one representative.

Functions and Powers

Article 62

1. The Economic and Social Council may make or initiate studies and reports with respect to international economic, social, cultural, educational, health, and related matters and may make recommendations with respect to any such matters to the General Assembly, to the Members of the United Nations, and to the specialized agencies concerned.

2. It may make recommendations for the purpose of promoting respect for, and observance of, human rights and fundamental freedoms for all.

3. It may prepare draft conventions for submission to the General Assembly, with respect to matters falling within its competence.

4. It may call, in accordance with the rules prescribed by the United Nations, international conferences on matters falling within its competence.

Article 63

1. The Economic and Social Council may enter into agreements with any of the agencies referred to in Article 57, defining the terms on which the agency concerned shall be brought into relationship with the United Nations. Such agreements shall be subject to approval by the General Assembly.

2. It may co-ordinate the activities of the specialized agencies through consultation with and recommendations to such agencies and through recommendations to the General Assembly and to the Members of the United Nations.

Article 64

1. The Economic and Social Council may take appropriate steps to obtain regular reports from the specialized agencies. It may make arrangements with the Members of the United Nations and with the specialized agencies to obtain reports on the steps taken to give effect to its own recommendations and to recommendations on matters falling within its competence made by the General Assembly.

2. It may communicate its observations on these reports to the General Assembly.

Article 65

The Economic and Social Council may furnish information to the Security Council and shall assist the Security Council upon its request.

Article 66

1. The Economic and Social Council shall perform such functions as fall within its competence in connexion with the carrying out of the recommendations of the General Assembly.

2. It may, with the approval of the General Assembly, perform services at the request of Members of the United Nations and at the request of specialized agencies.

3. It shall perform such other functions as are specified elsewhere in the present Charter or as may be assigned to it by the General Assembly.

Voting

Article 67

1. Each member of the Economic and Social Council shall have one vote.

2. Decisions of the Economic and Social Council shall be made by a majority of the members present and voting.

Procedure

Article 68

The Economic and Social Council shall set up commissions in economic and social fields and for the promotion of human rights, and such other commissions as may be required for the performance of its functions.

Article 69

The Economic and Social Council shall invite any Member of the United Nations to participate, without vote, in its deliberations on any matter of particular concern to that Member.

Article 70
The Economic and Social Council may make arrangements for representatives of the specialized agencies to participate, without vote, in its deliberations and in those of the commissions established by it, and for its representatives to participate in the deliberations of the specialized agencies.

Article 71
The Economic and Social Council may make suitable arrangements for consultation with non-governmental organizations which are concerned with matters within its competence. Such arrangements may be made with international organizations and, where appropriate, with national organizations after consultation with the Member of the United Nations concerned.

Article 72
1. The Economic and Social Council shall adopt its own rules of procedure, including the method of selecting its President.
2. The Economic and Social Council shall meet as required in accordance with its rules, which shall include provision for the convening of meetings on the request of a majority of its members.

CHAPTER XI
DECLARATION REGARDING NON-SELF-GOVERNING TERRITORIES

Article 73
Members of the United Nations which have or assume responsibilities for the administration of territories whose peoples have not yet attained a full measure of self-government recognize the principle that the interests of the inhabitants of these territories are paramount, and accept as a sacred trust the obligation to promote to the utmost, within the system of international peace and security established by the present Charter, the well-being of the inhabitants of these territories, and, to this end:

(a) to ensure, with due respect for the culture of the peoples concerned, their political, economic, social, and educational advancement, their just treatment, and their protection against abuses;

(b) to develop self-government, to take due account of the political aspirations of the peoples, and to assist them in the progressive development of their free political institutions, according to the particular circumstances of each territory and its peoples and their varying stages of advancement;

(c) to further international peace and security;

(d) to promote constructive measures of development, to encourage research, and to co-operate with one another and, when and where appropriate, with specialized international bodies with a view to the practical achievement of the social, economic, and scientific purposes set forth in this Article; and

(e) to transmit regularly to the Secretary-General for information purposes, subject to such limitation as security and constitutional considerations may require, statistical and other information of a technical nature relating to economic, social, and educational conditions in the territories for which they are respectively responsible other than those territories to which Chapters XII and XIII apply.

Article 74

Members of the United Nations also agree that their policy in respect of the territories to which this Chapter applies, no less than in respect of their metropolitan areas, must be based on the general principle of good neighbourliness, due account being taken of the interests and well-being of the rest of the world, in social, economic, and commercial matters.

CHAPTER XII
INTERNATIONAL TRUSTEESHIP SYSTEM

Article 75

The United Nations shall establish under its authority an international trusteeship system for the administration and supervision of such territories as may be placed thereunder by subsequent individual agreements. These territories are hereinafter referred to as trust territories.

Article 76

The basic objectives of the trusteeship system, in accordance with the Purposes of the United Nations laid down in Article 1 of the present Charter, shall be:

(a) to further international peace and security;

(b) to promote the political, economic, social, and educational advancement of the inhabitants of the trust territories, and their progressive development towards self-government or independence as may be appropriate to the particular circumstances of each territory and its peoples and the freely expressed wishes of the peoples concerned, and as may be provided by the terms of each trusteeship agreement;

(c) to encourage respect for human rights and for fundamental freedoms for all without distinction as to race, sex, language, or religion, and to encourage recognition of the interdependence of the peoples of the world; and

(d) to ensure equal treatment in social, economic, and commercial matters for all Members of the United Nations and their nationals, and also equal treatment for the latter in the administration of justice, without prejudice to the attainment of the foregoing objectives and subject to the provisions of Article 80.

Article 77

1. The trusteeship system shall apply to such territories in the following categories as may be placed thereunder by means of trusteeship agreements:

(a) territories now held under mandate

(b) territories which may be detached from enemy states as a result of the Second World War; and

(c) territories voluntarily placed under the system by states responsible for their administration.

2. It will be a matter for subsequent agreement as to which territories in the foregoing categories will be brought under the trusteeship system and upon what terms.

Article 78

The trusteeship system shall not apply to territories which have become Members of the United Nations, relationship among which shall be based on respect for the principle of sovereign equality.

Article 79

The terms of trusteeship for each territory to be placed under the trusteeship system, including any alteration or amendment, shall be agreed upon by the states directly concerned, including the mandatory power in the case of territories held under mandate by a Member of the United Nations, and shall be approved as provided for in Articles 83 and 85.

Article 80

1. Except as may be agreed upon in individual trusteeship agreements, made under Articles 77, 79, and 81, placing each territory under the trusteeship system, and until such agreements have been concluded, nothing in this Chapter shall be construed in or of itself to alter in any manner the rights whatsoever of any states or any peoples or the terms of existing international instruments to which Members of the United Nations may respectively be parties.

2. Paragraph 1 of this Article shall not be interpreted as giving grounds for delay or postponement of the negotiation and conclusion of agreements for placing mandated and other territories under the trusteeship system as provided for in Article 77.

Article 81

The trusteeship agreement shall in each case include the terms under which the trust territory will be administered and designate the authority which will exercise the administration of the trust territory. Such authority, hereinafter called the administering authority, may be one or more states or the Organization itself.

Article 82

There may be designated, in any trusteeship agreement, a strategic area or areas which may include part or all of the trust territory to which the agreement applies, without prejudice to any special agreement or agreements made under Article 43.

Article 83

1. All functions of the United Nations relating to strategic areas, including the approval of the terms of the trusteeship agreements and of their alternation or amendment, shall be exercised by the Security Council.

2. The basic objectives set forth in Article 76 shall be applicable to the people of each strategic area.

3. The Security Council shall, subject to the provisions of the trusteeship agreements and without prejudice to security considerations, avail itself of the assistance of the Trusteeship Council to perform those functions of the United Nations under the trusteeship system relating to political, economic, social, and educational matters in the strategic areas.

Article 84

It shall be the duty of the administering authority to ensure that the trust territory shall play its part in the maintenance of international peace and security. To this end the administering authority may make use of volunteer forces, facilities, and assistance from the trust territory in carrying out the obligations towards the Security Council undertaken in this regard by the administering authority, as well as for local defence and the maintenance of law and order within the trust territory.

Article 85

1. The functions of the United Nations with regard to trusteeship agreements for all areas not designated as strategic, including the approval of the terms of the trusteeship agreements and of their alteration or amendment, shall be exercised by the General Assembly.

2. The Trusteeship Council, operating under the authority of the General Assembly, shall assist the General Assembly in carrying out these functions.

CHAPTER XIII
THE TRUSTEESHIP COUNCIL

Composition

Article 86

1. The Trusteeship Council shall consist of the following Members of the United Nations:

(a) those Members administering trust territories;

(b) such of those Members mentioned by name in Article 23 as are not administering trust territories; and

(c) as many other Members elected for three-year terms by the General Assembly as may be necessary to ensure that the total number of members of the Trusteeship Council is equally divided between those Members of the United Nations which administer trust territories and those which do not.

2. Each member of the Trusteeship Council shall designate one specially qualified person to represent it therein.

Functions and Powers

Article 87

The General Assembly and, under its authority, the Trusteeship Council, in carrying out their functions, may:

(a) consider reports submitted by the administering authority;

(b) accept petitions and examine them in consultation with the administering authority;

(c) provide for periodic visits to the respective trust territories at times agreed upon with the administering authority; and

(d) take these and other actions in conformity with the terms of the trusteeship agreements.

Article 88

The Trusteeship Council shall formulate a questionnaire on the political, economic, social, and educational advancement of the inhabitants of each trust territory, and the administering authority for each trust territory within the competence of the General Assembly shall make an annual report to the General Assembly upon the basis of such questionnaire.

Voting

Article 89

1. Each member of the Trusteeship Council shall have one vote.

2. Decisions of the Trusteeship Council shall be made by a majority of the members present and voting.

Procedure

Article 90

1. The Trusteeship Council shall adopt its own rules of procedure, including the method of selecting its President.

2. The Trusteeship Council shall meet as required in accordance with its rules, which shall include provision for the convening of meetings on the request of a majority of its members.

Article 91

The Trusteeship Council shall, when appropriate, avail itself of the assistance of the Economic and Social Council and of the specialized agencies in regard to matters with which they are respectively concerned.

CHAPTER XIV
THE INTERNATIONAL COURT OF JUSTICE

Article 92

The International Court of Justice shall be the principal judicial organ of the United Nations. It shall function in accordance with the annexed Statute, which is based upon the Statute of the Permanent Court of International Justice and forms an integral part of the present Charter.

Article 93

1. All members of the United Nations are *ipso facto* parties to the Statute of the International Court of Justice.

2. A state which is not a Member of the United Nations may become a party to the Statute of the International Court of Justice on conditions to be determined in each case by the General Assembly upon the recommendation of the Security Council.

Article 94

1. Each member of the United Nations undertakes to comply with the decision of the International Court of Justice in any case to which it is a party.

2. If any party to a case fails to perform the obligations incumbent upon it under a judgment rendered by the Court, the other party may have recourse to the Security Council, which may, if it deems necessary, make recommendations or decide upon measures to be taken to give effect to the judgment.

Article 95

Nothing in the present Charter shall prevent Members of the United Nations from entrusting the solution of their differences to other tribunals by virtue of agreements already in existence or which may be concluded in the future.

Article 96

1. The General Assembly or the Security Council may request the International Court of Justice to give an advisory opinion on any legal question.

2. Other organs of the United Nations and specialized agencies, which may at any time be so authorized by the General Assembly, may also request advisory opinions of the Court on legal questions arising within the scope of their activities.

CHAPTER XV
THE SECRETARIAT

Article 97

The Secretariat shall comprise a Secretary-General and such staff as the Organization may require. The Secretary-General shall be appointed by the General Assembly upon the recommendation of the Security Council. He shall be the chief administrative officer of the Organization.

Article 98

The Secretary-General shall act in that capacity in all meetings of the General Assembly, of the Security Council, of the Economic and Social Council, and of the Trusteeship Council, and shall perform such other functions as are entrusted to him by these organs. The Secretary-General shall make an annual report to the General Assembly on the work of the Organization.

Article 99

The Secretary-General may bring to the attention of the Security Council any matter which in his opinion may threaten the maintenance of international peace and security.

Article 100

1. In the performance of their duties the Secretary-General and the staff shall not seek or receive instructions from any government or from any other authority external to the Organization. They shall refrain from any action which might reflect on their position as international officials responsible only to the Organization.

2. Each member of the United Nations undertakes to respect the exclusively international character of the responsibilities of the Secretary-General and the staff and not to seek to influence them in the discharge of their responsibilities.

Article 101

1. The staff shall be appointed by the Secretary-General under regulations established by the General Assembly.

2. Appropriate staffs shall be permanently assigned to the Economic and Social Council, the Trusteeship Council, and, as required, to other organs of the United Nations. These staffs shall form a part of the Secretariat.

3. The paramount consideration in the employment of the staff and in the determination of the conditions of service shall be the necessity of securing the highest standards of efficiency, competence, and integrity. Due regard shall be paid to the importance of recruiting the staff on as wide a geographical basis as possible.

CHAPTER XVI
MISCELLANEOUS PROVISIONS

Article 102

1. Every treaty and every international agreement entered into by any Member of the United Nations after the present Charter comes into force shall as soon as possible be registered with the Secretariat and published by it.

2. No party to any such treaty or international agreement which has not been registered in accordance with the provisions of paragraph 1 of this Article may invoke that treaty or agreement before any organ of the United Nations.

Article 103

In the event of a conflict between the obligations of the Members of the United Nations under the present Charter and their obligations under any other international agreement, their obligations under the present Charter shall prevail.

Article 104

The Organization shall enjoy in the territory of each of its Members such legal capacity as may be necessary for the exercise of its functions and the fulfilment of its purposes.

Article 105

1. The Organization shall enjoy in the territory of each of its Members such privileges and immunities as are necessary for the fulfilment of its purposes.

2. Representatives of the Members of the United Nations and officials of the Organization shall similarly enjoy such privileges and immunities as are necessary for the independent exercise of their functions in connexion with the Organization.

3. The General Assembly may make recommendations with a view to determining the details of the application of paragraphs 1 and 2 of this Article or may propose conventions to the Members of the United Nations for this purpose.

CHAPTER XVII
TRANSITIONAL SECURITY ARRANGEMENTS

Article 106

Pending the coming into force of such special agreements referred to in Article 43 as in the opinion of the Security Council enable it to begin the exercise of its responsibilities under Article 42, the parties to the Four-Nation Declaration, signed at Moscow, 30 October 1943, and France, shall, in accordance with the provisions of paragraph 5 of that Declaration, consult with one another and as occasion requires with other Members of the United Nations with a view to such joint action on behalf of the Organization as may be necessary for the purpose of maintaining international peace and security.

Article 107

Nothing in the present Charter shall invalidate or preclude action, in relation to any state which during the Second World War has been an enemy of any signatory to the present Charter, taken or authorized as a result of that war by the Governments having responsibility for such action.

CHAPTER XVIII
AMENDMENTS

Article 108

Amendments to the present Charter shall come into force for all Members of the United Nations when they have been adopted by a vote of two thirds of the members of the General Assembly and ratified in accordance with their respective constitutional processes by two thirds of the Members of the United Nations, including all the permanent members of the Security Council.

Article 109

1. A General Conference of the Members of the United Nations for the purpose of reviewing the present Charter may be held at a date and place to be fixed by a two-thirds vote of the members of the General Assembly and by a vote of any nine members of the Security Council. Each Member of the United Nations shall have one vote in the conference.

2. Any alteration of the present Charter recommended by a two-thirds vote of the conference shall take effect when ratified in accordance with their respective constitutional processes by two thirds of the Members of the United Nations including all the permanent members of the Security Council.

3. If such a conference has not been held before the tenth annual session of the General Assembly following the coming into force of the present Charter, the proposal to call such a conference shall be placed on the agenda of that session of the General Assembly, and the conference shall be held if so decided by a majority vote of the members of the General Assembly and by a vote of any seven members of the Security Council.

CHAPTER XIX
RATIFICATION AND SIGNATURE

Article 110

1. The present Charter shall be ratified by the signatory states in accordance with their respective constitutional processes.

2. The ratifications shall be deposited with the Government of the United States of America, which shall notify all the signatory states of each deposit as well as the Secretary-General of the Organization when he has been appointed.

3. The present Charter shall come into force upon the deposit of ratifications by the Republic of China, France, the Union of Soviet Socialist Republics, the United Kingdom of Great Britain and Northern Ireland, and the United States of America, and by a majority of the other signatory states. A protocol of the ratifications deposited shall thereupon be drawn up by the Government of the United States of America which shall communicate copies thereof to all the signatory states.

4. The states signatory to the present Charter which ratify it after it has come into force will become original Members of the United Nations on the date of the deposit of their respective ratifications.

Article 111

The present Charter, of which the Chinese, French, Russian, English, and Spanish texts are equally authentic, shall remain deposited in the archives of the Government of the United States of America. Duly certified copies thereof shall be transmitted by that Government to the governments of the other signatory states.

II
Declaration on Principles of International Law Concerning Friendly Relations and Co-operation among States in Accordance with the Charter of the United Nations

UNGA Res. 2625 (XXV), UN GAOR, 25th Sess., Supp. No. 28, at 121,
UN Doc. A/8028 (1971), adopted by consensus on October 24, 1970

The General Assembly,

Reaffirming in the terms of the Charter of the United Nations that the maintenance of international peace and security and the development of friendly relations and co-operation between nations are among the fundamental purposes of the United Nations,

Recalling that the peoples of the United Nations are determined to practise tolerance and live together in peace with one another as good neighbours,

Bearing in mind the importance of maintaining and strengthening international peace founded upon freedom, equality, justice and respect for fundamental human rights and of developing friendly relations among nations irrespective of their political, economic and social systems or the levels of their development,

Bearing in mind also the paramount importance of the Charter of the United Nations in the promotion of the rule of law among nations,

Considering that the faithful observance of the principles of international law concerning friendly relations and co-operation among States and the fulfilment in good faith of the obligations assumed by States, in accordance with the Charter, is of the greatest importance for the maintenance of international peace and security and for the implementation of the other purposes of the United Nations,

Noting that the great political, economic and social changes and scientific progress which have taken place in the world since the adoption of the Charter give increased importance to these principles and to the need for their more effective application in the conduct of States wherever carried on,

Recalling the established principle that outer space, including the Moon and other celestial bodies, is not subject to national appropriation by claim of sovereignty, by means of use or occupation, or by any other means, and mindful of the fact that consideration is being given in the United Nations to the question of establishing other appropriate provisions similarly inspired,

Convinced that the strict observance by States of the obligation not to intervene in the affairs of any other State is an essential condition to ensure that nations live together in peace with one another, since the practice of any form of intervention not only violates the spirit and letter of the Charter, but also leads to the creation of situations which threaten international peace and security,

Recalling the duty of States to refrain in their international relations from military, political, economic or any other form of coercion aimed against the political independence or territorial integrity of any State,

Considering it essential that all States shall refrain in their international relations from the threat or use of force against the territorial integrity or political independence of any State, or in any other manner inconsistent with the purposes of the United Nations,

Considering it equally essential that all States shall settle their international disputes by peaceful means in accordance with the Charter,

Reaffirming, in accordance with the Charter, the basic importance of sovereign equality and stressing that the purposes of the United Nations can be implemented only if States enjoy sovereign equality and comply fully with the requirements of this principle in their international relations,

Convinced that the subjection of peoples to alien subjugation, domination and exploitation constitutes a major obstacle to the promotion of international peace and security,

Convinced that the principle of equal rights and self-determination of peoples constitutes a significant contribution to contemporary international law, and that its effective application is of paramount importance for the promotion of friendly relations among States, based on respect for the principle of sovereign equality,

Convinced in consequence that any attempt aimed at the partial or total disruption of the national unity and territorial integrity of a State or country or at its political independence is incompatible with the purposes and principles of the Charter,

Considering the provisions of the Charter as a whole and taking into account the role of relevant resolutions adopted by the competent organs of the United Nations relating to the content of the principles,

Considering that the progressive development and codification of the following principles:

(a) The principle that States shall refrain in their international relations from the threat or use of force against the territorial integrity or political independence of any State, or in any other manner inconsistent with the purposes of the United Nations,

(b) The principle that States shall settle their international disputes by peaceful means in such a manner that international peace and security and justice are not endangered,

(c) The duty not to intervene in matters within the domestic jurisdiction of any state, in accordance with the Charter,

(d) The duty of States to co-operate with one another in accordance with the Charter,

(e) The principle of equal rights and self-determination of peoples,

(f) The principle of sovereign equality of States,

(g) The principle that States shall fulfill in good faith the obligations assumed by them in accordance with the Charter, so as to secure their more effective application within the international community, would promote the realization of the purposes of the United Nations.

Having considered the principles of international law relating to friendly relations and co-operation among States,

1. *Solemnly proclaims* the following principles:

The principle that States shall refrain in their international relations from the threat or use of force against the territorial integrity or political independence of any State, or in any other manner inconsistent with the purposes of the United Nations

Every State has the duty to refrain in its international relations from the threat or use of force against the territorial integrity or political independence of any State, or in any other manner inconsistent with the purposes of the United Nations. Such a threat or use of force constitutes a violation of international law and the Charter of the United Nations and shall never be employed as a means of settling international issues.

A war of aggression constitutes a crime against the peace, for which there is responsibility under international law.

In accordance with the purposes and principles of the United Nations, States have the duty to refrain from propaganda for wars of aggression.

Every State has the duty to refrain from the threat or use of force to violate the existing international boundaries of another State or as a means of solving international disputes, including territorial disputes and problems concerning frontiers of States.

Every State likewise has the duty to refrain from the threat or use of force to violate international lines of demarcation, such as armistice lines, established by or pursuant to an international agreement to which it is a party or which it is otherwise bound to respect. Nothing in the foregoing shall be construed as prejudicing the positions of the parties concerned with regard to the status and effects of such lines under their special régimes or as affecting their temporary character.

States have a duty to refrain from acts of reprisal involving the use of force.

Every State has the duty to refrain from any forcible action which deprives peoples referred to in the elaboration of the principle of equal rights and self-determination of their right to self-determination and freedom and independence.

Every State has the duty to refrain from organizing or encouraging the organization of irregular forces or armed bands, including mercenaries, for incursion into the territory of another State.

Every State has the duty to refrain from organizing, instigating, assisting or participating in acts of civil strife or terrorist acts in another State or acquiescing in organized activities within its territory directed towards the commission of such acts, when the acts referred to in the present paragraph involve a threat or use of force.

The territory of a State shall not be the object of military occupation resulting from the use of force in contravention of the provisions of the Charter. The territory of a State shall not be the object of acquisition by another State resulting from the threat or use of force. No territorial acquisition resulting from the threat or use of force shall be recognized as legal. Nothing in the foregoing shall be construed as affecting:

(a) Provisions of the Charter or any international agreement prior to the Charter regime and valid under international law; or

(b) The powers of the Security Council under the Charter.

All States shall pursue in good faith negotiations for the early conclusion of a universal treaty on general and complete disarmament under effective international control and strive to adopt appropriate measures to reduce international tensions and strengthen confidence among States.

All States shall comply in good faith with their obligations under the generally recognized principles and rules of international law with respect to the maintenance of international peace and security, and shall endeavour to make the United Nations security system based on the Charter more effective.

Nothing in the foregoing paragraphs shall be construed as enlarging or diminishing in any way the scope of the provisions of the Charter concerning cases in which the use of force is lawful.

The principle that States shall settle their international disputes by peaceful means in such a manner that international peace and security and justice are not endangered

Every State shall settle its international disputes with other States by peaceful means in such a manner that international peace and security and justice are not endangered.

States shall accordingly seek early and just settlement of their international disputes by negotiation, inquiry, mediation, conciliation, arbitration, judicial settlement, resort to regional agencies or arrangements or other peaceful means of their choice. In seeking such a settlement the parties shall agree upon such peaceful means as may be appropriate to the circumstances and nature of the dispute.

The parties to a dispute have the duty, in the event of failure to reach a solution by any one of the above peaceful means, to continue to seek a settlement of the dispute by other peaceful means agreed upon by them.

States parties to an international dispute, as well as other States, shall refrain from any action which may aggravate the situation so as to endanger the maintenance of international peace and security, and shall act in accordance with the purposes and principles of the United Nations.

International disputes shall be settled on the basis of the sovereign equality of States and in accordance with the principle of free choice of means. Recourse to, or acceptance of, a settlement procedure freely agreed to by States with regard to existing or future disputes to which they are parties shall not be regarded as incompatible with sovereign equality.

Nothing in the foregoing paragraphs prejudices or derogates from the applicable provisions of the Charter, in particular those relating to the pacific settlement of international disputes.

The principle concerning the duty not to intervene in matters within the domestic jurisdiction of any State, in accordance with the Charter

No State or group of States has the right to intervene, directly or indirectly, for any reason whatever, in the internal or external affairs of any other State. Consequently, armed intervention and all other forms of interference or attempted threats against the personality of the State or against its political, economic and cultural elements, are in violation of international law.

No State may use or encourage the use of economic, political or any other type of measures to coerce another State in order to obtain from it the subordination of the exercise of its sovereign rights and to secure from it advantages of any kind. Also, no State shall organize, assist, foment, finance, incite or tolerate subversive, terrorist or armed activities directed towards the violent overthrow of the regime of another State, or interfere in civil strife in another State.

The use of force to deprive peoples of their national identity constitutes a violation of their inalienable rights and of the principle of non-intervention.

Every State has an inalienable right to choose its political, economic, social and cultural systems, without interference in any form by another State.

Nothing in the foregoing paragraphs shall be construed as affecting the relevant provisions of the Charter relating to the maintenance of international peace and security.

The duty of States to co-operate with one another in accordance with the Charter

States have the duty to co-operate with one another, irrespective of the differences in their political, economic and social systems, in the various spheres of international relations, in order to maintain international peace and security and to promote international economic stability and progress, the general welfare of nations and international co-operation free from discrimination based on such differences.

To this end:

(a) States shall co-operate with other States in the maintenance of international peace and security;

(b) States shall co-operate in the promotion of universal respect for, and observance of, human rights and fundamental freedoms for all, and in the elimination of all forms of racial discrimination and all forms of religious intolerance;

(c) States shall conduct their international relations in the economic, social, cultural, technical and trade fields in accordance with the principles of sovereign equality and non-intervention;

(d) States Members of the United Nations have the duty to take joint and separate action in co-operation with the United Nations in accordance with the relevant provisions of the Charter.

States should co-operate in the economic, social and cultural fields as well as in the field of science and technology and for the promotion of international cultural and educational progress. States should co-operate in the promotion of economic growth throughout the world, especially that of the developing countries.

The principle of equal rights and self-determination of peoples

By virtue of the principle of equal rights and self-determination of peoples enshrined in the Charter of the United Nations, all peoples have the right freely to determine, without external interference, their political status and to pursue their economic, social and cultural development, and every State has the duty to respect this right in accordance with the provisions of the Charter.

Every State has the duty to promote, through joint and separate action, realization of the principle of equal rights and self-determination of peoples, in accordance with the provisions of the Charter, and to render assistance to the United Nations in carrying out the responsibilities entrusted to it by the Charter regarding the implementation of the principle, in order:

(a) To promote friendly relations and co-operation among States; and

(b) To bring a speedy end of colonialism, having due regard to the freely expressed will of the peoples concerned;

and bearing in mind that subjection of peoples to alien subjugation, domination and exploitation constitutes a violation of the principle, as well as a denial of fundamental human rights, and is contrary to the Charter.

Every State has the duty to promote through joint and separate action universal respect for and observance of human rights and fundamental freedoms in accordance with the Charter.

The establishment of a sovereign and independent State, the free association or integration with an independent State or the emergence into any other political status freely determined by a people constitute modes of implementing the right of self-determination by that people.

Every State has the duty to refrain from any forcible action which deprives peoples referred to above in the elaboration of the present principle of their right to self-determination and freedom and independence. In their actions against, and resistance to, such forcible action in pursuit of the exercise of their right to self-determination, such peoples are entitled to seek and to receive support in accordance with the purposes and principles of the Charter.

The territory of a colony or other Non-Self-Governing Territory has, under the Charter, a status separate and distinct from the territory of the State administering it; and such separate and distinct status under the Charter shall exist until the people of the colony or Non-Self-Governing Territory have exercised their right of self-determination in accordance with the Charter, and particularly its purposes and principles.

Nothing in the foregoing paragraphs shall be construed as authorizing or encouraging any action which would dismember or impair, totally or in part, the territorial integrity or political unity of sovereign and independent States conducting themselves in compliance with the principle of equal rights and self-determination of peoples as described above and thus possessed of a government representing the whole people belonging to the territory without distinction as to race, creed or colour.

Every State shall refrain from any action aimed at the partial or total disruption of the national unity and territorial integrity of any other State or country.

The principle of sovereign equality of States

All States enjoy sovereign equality. They have equal rights and duties and are equal members of the international community, notwithstanding differences of an economic, social, political or other nature.

In particular, sovereign equality includes the following elements:

(a) States are judicially equal;

(b) Each State enjoys the rights inherent in full sovereignty;

(c) Each State has the duty to respect the personality of other States;

(d) The territorial integrity and political independence of the State are inviolable;

(e) Each State has the right freely to choose and develop its political, social, economic and cultural systems;

(f) Each State has the duty to comply fully and in good faith with its international obligations and to live in peace with other States.

The principle that States shall fulfill in good faith the obligations assumed by them in accordance with the Charter

Every State has the duty to fulfil in good faith the obligations assumed by it in accordance with the Charter of the United Nations.

Every State has the duty to fulfil in good faith its obligations under the generally recognized principles and rules of international law.

Every State has the duty to fulfil in good faith its obligations under international agreements valid under the generally recognized principles and rules of international law.

Where obligations arising under international agreements are in conflict with the obligations of Members of the United Nations under the Charter of the United Nations, the obligations under the Charter shall prevail.

GENERAL PART

2. *Declares* that:

In their interpretation and application the above principles are interrelated and each principle should be construed in the context of the other principles.

Nothing in this Declaration shall be construed as prejudicing in any manner the provisions of the Charter or the rights and duties of Member States under the Charter or the rights of peoples under the Charter, taking into account the elaboration of these rights in this Declaration.

3. *Declares further* that:

The principles of the Charter which are embodied in this Declaration constitute basic principles of international law, and consequently appeals to all States to be guided by these principles in their international conduct and to develop their mutual relations on the basis of the strict observance of these principles.

III
Statute of the International Court of Justice

As signed 1945

Article 1

THE INTERNATIONAL COURT OF JUSTICE established by the Charter of the United Nations as the principal judicial organ of the United Nations shall be constituted and shall function in accordance with the provisions of the present Statute.

CHAPTER I
ORGANIZATION OF THE COURT

Article 2

The Court shall be composed of a body of independent judges, elected regardless of their nationality from among persons of high moral character, who possess the qualifications required in their respective countries for appointment to the highest judicial offices, or are jurisconsults of recognized competence in international law.

Article 3

1. The Court shall consist of fifteen members, no two of whom may be nationals of the same State.

2. A person who for the purposes of membership in the Court could be regarded as a national of more than one State shall be deemed to be a national of the one in which he ordinarily exercises civil and political rights.

Article 4

1. The members of the Court shall be elected by the General Assembly and by the Security Council from a list of persons nominated by the national groups in the Permanent Court of Arbitration, in accordance with the following provisions.

2. In the case of Members of the United Nations not represented in the Permanent Court of Arbitration, candidates shall be nominated by national groups appointed for this purpose by their governments under the same conditions as those prescribed for members of the Permanent Court of Arbitration by Article 44 of the Convention of The Hague of 1907 for the pacific settlement of international disputes.

3. The conditions under which a State which is a party to the present Statute but is not a Member of the United Nations may participate in electing the members of the Court shall, in the absence of a special agreement, be laid down by the General Assembly upon recommendation of the Security Council.

Article 5

1. At least three months before the date of the election, the Secretary-General of the United Nations shall address a written request to the members of the Permanent Court of Arbitration belonging to the States which are parties to the present Statute, and to the members of the national groups appointed under Article 4, paragraph 2, inviting them to undertake, within

33

a given time, by national groups, the nomination of persons in a position to accept the duties of a member of the Court.

2. No group may nominate more than four persons, not more than two of whom shall be of their own nationality. In no case may the number of candidates nominated by a group be more than double the number of seats to be filled.

Article 6

Before making these nominations, each national group is recommended to consult its highest court of justice, its legal faculties and schools of law, and its national academies and national sections of international academies devoted to the study of law.

Article 7

1. The Secretary-General shall prepare a list in alphabetical order of all the persons thus nominated. Save as provided in Article 12, paragraph 2, these shall be the only persons eligible.

2. The Secretary-General shall submit this list to the General Assembly and to the Security Council.

Article 8

The General Assembly and the Security Council shall proceed independently of one another to elect the members of the Court.

Article 9

At every election, the electors shall bear in mind not only that the persons to be elected should individually possess the qualifications required, but also that in the body as a whole the representation of the main forms of civilization and of the principal legal systems of the world should be assured.

Article 10

1. Those candidates who obtain an absolute majority of votes in the General Assembly and in the Security Council shall be considered as elected.

2. Any vote of the Security Council, whether for the election of judges or for the appointment of members of the conference envisaged in Article 12, shall be taken without any distinction between permanent and non-permanent members of the Security Council.

3. In the event of more than one national of the same State obtaining an absolute majority of the votes both of the General Assembly and of the Security Council, the eldest of these only shall be considered as elected.

Article 11

If, after the first meeting held for the purpose of the election, one or more seats remain to be filled, a second and, if necessary, a third meeting shall take place.

Article 12

1. If, after the third meeting, one or more seats still remain unfilled, a joint conference consisting of six members, three appointed by the General Assembly and three by the

Security Council, may be formed at any time at the request of either the General Assembly or the Security Council, for the purpose of choosing by the vote of an absolute majority one name for each seat still vacant, to submit to the General Assembly and the Security Council for their respective acceptance.

2. If the joint conference is unanimously agreed upon any person who fulfils the required conditions, he may be included in its list, even though he was not included in the list of nominations referred to in Article 7.

3. If the joint conference is satisfied that it will not be successful in procuring an election, those members of the Court who have already been elected shall, within a period to be fixed by the Security Council, proceed to fill the vacant seats by selection from among those candidates who have obtained votes either in the General Assembly or in the Security Council.

4. In the event of an equality of votes among the judges, the eldest judge shall have a casting vote.

Article 13

1. The members of the Court shall be elected for nine years and may be re-elected; provided, however, that of the judges elected at the first election, the terms of five judges shall expire at the end of three years and the terms of five more judges shall expire at the end of six years.

2. The judges whose terms are to expire at the end of the above-mentioned initial periods of three and six years shall be chosen by lot to be drawn by the Secretary-General immediately after the first election has been completed.

3. The members of the Court shall continue to discharge their duties until their places have been filled. Though replaced, they shall finish any cases which they may have begun.

4. In the case of the resignation of a member of the Court, the resignation shall be addressed to the President of the Court for transmission to the Secretary-General. This last notification makes the place vacant.

Article 14

Vacancies shall be filled by the same method as that laid down for the first election, subject to the following provision: the Secretary-General shall, within one month of the occurrence of the vacancy, proceed to issue the invitations provided for in Article 5, and the date of the election shall be fixed by the Security Council.

Article 15

A member of the Court elected to replace a member whose term of office has not expired shall hold office for the remainder of his predecessor's term.

Article 16

1. No member of the Court may exercise any political or administrative function, or engage in any other occupation of a professional nature.

2. Any doubt on this point shall be settled by the decision of the Court.

Article 17

1. No member of the Court may act as agent, counsel or advocate in any case.

2. No member may participate in the decision of any case in which he has previously taken part as agent, counsel or advocate for one of the parties, or as a member of a national or international court, or of a commission of enquiry, or in any other capacity.

3. Any doubt on this point shall be settled by the decision of the Court.

Article 18

1. No member of the Court can be dismissed unless, in the unanimous opinion of the other members, he has ceased to fulfil the required conditions.

2. Formal notification thereof shall be made to the Secretary-General by the Registrar.

3. This notification makes the place vacant.

Article 19

The members of the court, when engaged on the business of the Court, shall enjoy diplomatic privileges and immunities.

Article 20

Every member of the Court shall, before taking up his duties, make a solemn declaration in open Court that he will exercise his powers impartially and conscientiously.

Article 21

1. The Court shall elect its President and Vice-President for three years; they may be re-elected.

2. The Court shall appoint its Registrar and may provide for the appointment of such other officers as may be necessary.

Article 22

1. The seat of the Court shall be established at The Hague. This, however, shall not prevent the Court from sitting and exercising its functions elsewhere whenever the Court considers it desirable.

2. The President and the Registrar shall reside at the seat of the Court.

Article 23

1. The Court shall remain permanently in session, except during the judicial vacations, the dates and duration of which shall be fixed by the Court.

2. Members of the Court are entitled to periodic leave, the dates and duration of which shall be fixed by the Court, having in mind the distance between The Hague and the home of each judge.

3. Members of the Court shall be bound, unless they are on leave or prevented from attending by illness or other serious reasons duly explained to the President, to hold themselves permanently at the disposal of the Court.

Article 24

1. If, for some special reason, a member of the Court considers that he should not take part in the decision of a particular case, he shall so inform the President.

2. If the President considers that for some reason one of the members of the Court should not sit in a particular case, he shall give him notice accordingly.

3. If in any such case the member of the Court and the President disagree, the matter shall be settled by the decision of the Court.

Article 25

1. The full Court shall sit except when it is expressly provided otherwise in the present Statute.

2. Subject to the condition that the number of judges available to constitute the Court is not thereby reduced below eleven, the Rules of the Court may provide for allowing one or more judges, according to circumstances and in rotation, to be dispensed from sitting.

3. A quorum of nine judges shall suffice to constitute the Court.

Article 26

1. The Court may from time to time form one or more Chambers, composed of three of more judges as the Court may determine, for dealing with particular categories of cases; for example, labour cases and cases relating to transit and communications.

2. The Court may at any time form a Chamber for dealing with a particular case. The number of judges to constitute such a Chamber shall be determined by the Court with the approval of the parties.

3. Cases shall be heard and determined by the Chambers provided for in this Article if the parties so request.

Article 27

A judgment given by any of the Chambers provided for in Articles 26 and 29 shall be considered as rendered by the Court.

Article 28

The Chambers provided for in Articles 26 and 29 may, with the consent of the parties, sit and exercise their functions elsewhere than at The Hague.

Article 29

With a view to the speedy dispatch of business, the Court shall form annually a Chamber composed of five judges which, at the request of the parties, may hear and determine cases by summary procedure. In addition, two judges shall be selected for the purpose of replacing judges who find it impossible to sit.

Article 30

1. The Court shall frame rules for carrying out its functions. In particular, it shall lay down rules of procedure.

2. The Rules of the Court may provide for assessors to sit with the Court or with any of its Chambers, without the right to vote.

Article 31

1. Judges of the nationality of each of the parties shall retain their right to sit in the case before the Court.

2. If the Court includes upon the Bench a judge of the nationality of one of the parties, any other party may choose a person to sit as judge. Such person shall be chosen preferably from among those persons who have been nominated as candidates as provided in Articles 4 and 5.

3. If the Court includes upon the Bench no judge of the nationality of the parties, each of these parties may proceed to choose a judge as provided in paragraph 2 of this Article.

4. The provisions of this Article shall apply to the case of Articles 26 and 29. In such cases, the President shall request one or, if necessary, two of the members of the Court forming the Chamber to give place to the members of the Court of the nationality of the parties concerned, and, failing such, or if they are unable to be present, to the judges specially chosen by the parties.

5. Should there be several parties in the same interest, they shall, for the purpose of the preceding provisions, be reckoned as one party only. Any doubt upon this point shall be settled by the decision of the Court.

6. Judges chosen as laid down in paragraphs 2, 3 and 4 of this Article shall fulfil the conditions required by Articles 2, 17 (paragraph 2), 20 and 24 of the present Statute. They shall take part in the decision on terms of complete equality with their colleagues.

Article 32

1. Each member of the Court shall receive an annual salary.

2. The President shall receive a special annual allowance.

3. The Vice-President shall receive a special allowance for every day on which he acts as President.

4. The judges chosen under Article 31, other than members of the Court, shall receive compensation for each day on which they exercise their functions.

5. These salaries, allowances and compensation shall be fixed by the General Assembly. They may not be decreased during the term of office.

6. The salary of the Registrar shall be fixed by the General Assembly on the proposal of the Court.

7. Regulations made by the General Assembly shall fix the conditions under which retirement pensions may be given to members of the Court and to the Registrar, and the conditions under which members of the Court and the Registrar shall have their travelling expenses refunded.

8. The above salaries, allowances and compensation shall be free of all taxation.

Article 33

The expenses of the Court shall be borne by the United Nations in such a manner as shall be decided by the General Assembly.

CHAPTER II
COMPETENCE OF THE COURT

Article 34

1. Only States may be parties in cases before the Court.

2. The Court, subject to and in conformity with its Rules, may request of public international organizations information relevant to cases before it, and shall receive such information presented by such organizations on their own initiative.

3. Whenever the construction of the constituent instrument of a public international organization or of an international convention adopted thereunder is in question in a case before the Court, the Registrar shall so notify the public international organization concerned and shall communicate to it copies of all the written proceedings.

Article 35

1. The Court shall be open to the States parties to the present Statute.

2. The conditions under which the Court shall be open to other States shall, subject to the special provisions contained in treaties in force, be laid down by the Security Council, but in no case shall such conditions place the parties in a position of inequality before the Court.

3. When a State which is not a Member of the United Nations is a party to a case, the Court shall fix the amount which that party is to contribute towards the expenses of the Court. This provision shall not apply if such State is bearing a share of the expenses of the Court.

Article 36

1. The jurisdiction of the Court comprises all cases which the parties refer to it and all matters specially provided for in the Charter of the United Nations or in treaties and conventions in force.

2. The States parties to the present Statute may at any time declare that they recognize as compulsory *ipso facto* and without special agreement, in relation to any other State accepting the same obligation, the jurisdiction of the Court in all legal disputes concerning:

(a) the interpretation of a treaty;

(b) any question of international law;

(c) the existence of any fact which, if established, would constitute a breach of an international obligation;

(d) the nature or extent of the reparation to be made for the breach of an international obligation.

3. The declarations referred to above may be made unconditionally or on condition of reciprocity on the part of several or certain States, or for a certain time.

4. Such declarations shall be deposited with the Secretary-General of the United Nations, who shall transmit copies thereof to the parties to the Statute and to the Registrar of the Court.

5. Declarations made under Article 36 of the Statute of the Permanent Court of International Justice and which are still in force shall be deemed, as between the parties to the present Statute, to be acceptances of the compulsory jurisdiction of the International Court of Justice for the period which they still have to run and in accordance with their terms.

6. In the event of a dispute as to whether the Court has jurisdiction, the matter shall be settled by the decision of the Court.

Article 37

Whenever a treaty or convention in force provides for reference of a matter to a tribunal to have been instituted by the League of Nations, or to the Permanent Court of International Justice, the matter shall, as between the parties to the present Statute, be referred to the International Court of Justice.

Article 38

1. The Court, whose function is to decide in accordance with international law such disputes as are submitted to it, shall apply:

(a) international conventions, whether general or particular, establishing rules expressly recognized by the contesting States;

(b) international custom, as evidence of a general practice accepted as law;

(c) the general principles of law recognized by civilized nations;

(d) subject to the provisions of Article 59, judicial decisions and the teachings of the most highly qualified publicists of the various nations, as subsidiary means for the determination of rules of law.

2. This provision shall not prejudice the power of the Court to decide a case *ex æquo et bono*, if the parties agree thereto.

CHAPTER III
PROCEDURE

Article 39

1. The official languages of the Court shall be French and English. If the parties agree that the case shall be conducted in French, the judgment shall be delivered in French. If the parties agree that the case shall be conducted in English, the judgment shall be delivered in English.

2. In the absence of an agreement as to which language shall be employed, each party may, in the pleadings, use the language which it prefers; the decision of the Court shall be given in French and English. In this case the Court shall at the same time determine which of the two texts shall be considered as authoritative.

3. The Court shall, at the request of any party, authorize a language other than French or English to be used by that party.

Article 40

1. Cases are brought before the Court, as the case may be, either by the notification of the special agreement or by a written application addressed to the Registrar. In either case the subject of the dispute and the parties shall be indicated.

2. The Registrar shall forthwith communicate the application to all concerned.

3. He shall also notify the Members of the United Nations through the Secretary-General, and also any other States entitled to appear before the Court.

Article 41

1. The Court shall have the power to indicate, if it considers that circumstances so require, any provisional measures which ought to be taken to preserve the respective rights of either party.

2. Pending the final decision, notice of the measures suggested shall forthwith be given to the parties and to the Security Council.

Article 42

1. The parties shall be represented by agents.

2. They may have the assistance of counsel or advocates before the Court.

3. The agents, counsel and advocates of parties before the Court shall enjoy the privileges and immunities necessary to the independent exercise of their duties.

Article 43

1. The procedure shall consist of two parts: written and oral.

2. The written proceedings shall consist of the communication to the Court and to the parties of Memorials, Counter-Memorials and, if necessary, Replies; also all papers and documents in support.

3. These communications shall be made through the Registrar, in the order and within the time fixed by the Court.

4. A certified copy of every document produced by one party shall be communicated to the other party.

5. The oral proceedings shall consist of the hearing by the Court of witnesses, experts, agents, counsel and advocates.

Article 44

1. For the service of all notices upon persons other than the agents, counsel and advocates, the Court shall apply direct to the government of the State upon whose territory the notice has to be served.

2. The same provision shall apply whenever steps are to be taken to procure evidence on the spot.

Article 45

The hearing shall be under the control of the President or, if he is unable to preside, of the Vice-President; if neither is able to preside, the senior judge present shall preside.

Article 46

The hearing in Court shall be public, unless the Court shall decide otherwise, or unless the parties demand that the public be not admitted.

Article 47

1. Minutes shall be made at each hearing and signed by the Registrar and the President.

2. These minutes alone shall be authentic.

Article 48

The Court shall make orders for the conduct of the case, shall decide the form and time in which each party must conclude its arguments, and make all arrangements connected with the taking of evidence.

Article 49

The Court may, even before the hearing begins, call upon the agents to produce any document or to supply any explanations. Formal note shall be taken of any refusal.

Article 50

The Court may, at any time, entrust any individual, body, bureau, commission or other organization that it may select, with the task of carrying out an enquiry or giving an expert opinion.

Article 51

During the hearing any relevant questions are to be put to the witnesses and experts under the conditions laid down by the Court in the rules of procedure referred to in Article 30.

Article 52

After the Court has received the proofs and evidence within the time specified for the purpose, it may refuse to accept any further oral or written evidence that one party may desire to present unless the other side consents.

Article 53

1. Whenever one of the parties does not appear before the Court, or fails to defend its case, the other party may call upon the Court to decide in favour of its claim.

2. The Court must, before doing so, satisfy itself, not only that it has jurisdiction in accordance with Articles 36 and 37, but also that the claim is well founded in fact and law.

Article 54

1. When, subject to the control of the Court, the agents, counsel and advocates have completed their presentation of the case, the President shall declare the hearing closed.

2. The Court shall withdraw to consider the judgment.

3. The deliberations of the Court shall take place in private and remain secret.

Article 55

1. All questions shall be decided by a majority of the judges present.

2. In the event of an equality of votes, the President or the judge who acts in his place shall have a casting vote.

Article 56

1. The judgment shall state the reasons on which it is based.

2. It shall contain the names of the judges who have taken part in the decision.

Article 57

If the judgment does not represent in whole or in part the unanimous opinion of the judges, any judge shall be entitled to deliver a separate opinion.

Article 58

The judgment shall be signed by the President and by the Registrar. It shall be read in open Court, due notice having been given to the agents.

Article 59

The decision of the Court has no binding force except between the parties and in respect of that particular case.

Article 60

The judgment is final and without appeal. In the event of dispute as to the meaning or scope of the judgment, the Court shall construe it upon the request of any party.

Article 61

1. An application for revision of a judgment may be made only when it is based upon the discovery of some fact of such a nature as to be a decisive factor, which fact was, when the judgment was given, unknown to the Court and also to the party claiming revision, always provided that such ignorance was not due to negligence.

2. The proceedings for revision shall be opened by a judgment of the Court expressly recording the existence of the new fact, recognizing that it has such a character as to lay the case open to revision, and declaring the application admissible on this ground.

3. The Court may require previous compliance with the terms of the judgment before it admits proceedings in revision.

4. The application for revision must be made at latest within six months of the discovery of the new fact.

5. No application for revision may be made after the lapse of ten years from the date of the judgment.

Article 62

1. Should a State consider that it has an interest of a legal nature which may be affected by the decision in the case, it may submit a request to the Court to be permitted to intervene.

2. It shall be for the Court to decide upon this request.

Article 63

1. Whenever the construction of a convention to which States other than those concerned in the case are parties is in question, the Registrar shall notify all such States forthwith.

2. Every State so notified has the right to intervene in the proceedings; but if it uses this right, the construction given by the judgment will be equally binding upon it.

Article 64

Unless otherwise decided by the Court, each party shall bear its own costs.

CHAPTER IV
ADVISORY OPINIONS

Article 65

1. The Court may give an advisory opinion on any legal question at the request of whatever body may be authorized by or in accordance with the Charter of the United Nations to make such a request.

2. Questions upon which the advisory opinion of the Court is asked shall be laid before the Court by means of a written request containing an exact statement of the question upon which an opinion is required, and accompanied by all documents likely to throw light upon the question.

Article 66

1. The Registrar shall forthwith give notice of the request for an advisory opinion to all States entitled to appear before the Court.

2. The Registrar shall also, by means of a special and direct communication, notify any State entitled to appear before the Court or international organization considered by the Court, or, should it not be sitting, by the President, as likely to be able to furnish information on the question, that the Court will be prepared to receive, within a time-limit to be fixed by the President, written statements, or to hear, at a public sitting to be held for the purpose, oral statements relating to the question.

3. Should any such State entitled to appear before the Court have failed to receive the special communication referred to in paragraph 2 of this Article, such State may express a desire to submit a written statement or to be heard; and the Court will decide.

4. States and organizations having presented written or oral statements or both shall be permitted to comment on the statements made by other States or organizations in the form, to the extent and within the time-limits which the Court, or, should it not be sitting, the President, shall decide in each particular case. Accordingly, the Registrar shall in due time communicate any such written statements to States and organizations having submitted similar statements.

Article 67

The Court shall deliver its advisory opinions in open Court, notice having been given to the Secretary-General and to the representatives of Members of the United Nations, of other States and of international organizations immediately concerned.

Article 68

In the exercise of its advisory functions, the Court shall further be guided by the provisions of the present Statute which apply in contentious cases to the extent to which it recognizes them to be applicable.

CHAPTER V
AMENDMENT

Article 69

Amendments to the present Statute shall be effected by the same procedure as is provided by the Charter of the United Nations for amendments to that Charter, subject however to any provisions which the General Assembly upon recommendation of the Security Council may adopt concerning the participation of States which are parties to the present Statute but are not Members of the United Nations.

Article 70

The Court shall have power to propose such amendments to the present Statute as it may deem necessary, through written communications to the Secretary-General, for consideration in conformity with the provisions of Article 69.

IV
Vienna Convention on the Law of Treaties

(1969) 1155 U.N.T.S. 331, in force 1980

PART I
INTRODUCTION

Article 1

Scope of the present Convention

The present Convention applies to treaties between States.

Article 2

Use of terms

1. For the purposes of the present Convention:

(a) "treaty" means an international agreement concluded between States in written form and governed by international law, whether embodied in a single instrument or in two or more related instruments and whatever its particular designation;

(b) "ratification", "acceptance", "approval" and "accession" mean in each case the international act so named whereby a State establishes on the international plane its consent to be bound by a treaty;

(c) "full powers" means a document emanating from the competent authority of a State designating a person or persons to represent the State for negotiating, adopting or authenticating the text of a treaty, for expressing the consent of the State to be bound by a treaty, or for accomplishing any other act with respect to a treaty;

(d) "reservation" means a unilateral statement, however phrased or named, made by a State, when signing, ratifying, accepting, approving or acceding to a treaty, whereby it purports to exclude or to modify the legal effect of certain provisions of the treaty in their application to that State;

(e) "negotiating State" means a State which took part in the drawing up and adoption of the text of the treaty;

(f) "contracting State" means a State which has consented to be bound by the treaty, whether or not the treaty has entered into force;

(g) "party" means a State which has consented to be bound by the treaty and for which the treaty is in force;

(h) "third State" means a State not a party to the treaty;

(i) "international organization" means an intergovernmental organization.

2. The provisions of paragraph 1 regarding the use of terms in the present Convention are without prejudice to the use of those terms or to the meanings which may be given to them in the internal law of any State.

Article 3

International agreements not within the scope of the present Convention

The fact that the present Convention does not apply to international agreements concluded

45

between states and other subjects of international law or between such other subjects of international law, or to international agreements not in written form, shall not affect:

(a) the legal force of such agreements;

(b) the application to them of any of the rules set forth in the present Convention to which they would be subject under international law independently of the Convention;

(c) the application of the Convention to the relations of states as between themselves under international agreements to which other subjects of international law are also parties.

Article 4

Non-retroactivity of the present Convention

Without prejudice to the application of any rules set forth in the present Convention to which treaties would be subject under international law independently of the Convention, the Convention applies only to treaties which are concluded by states after the entry into force of the present Convention with regard to such states.

Article 5

Treaties constituting international organizations and treaties adopted within an international organization

The present Convention applies to any treaty which is the constituent instrument of an international organization and to any treaty adopted within an international organization without prejudice to any relevant rules of the organization.

PART II
CONCLUSION AND ENTRY INTO FORCE OF TREATIES

SECTION 1. CONCLUSION OF TREATIES

Article 6

Capacity of states to conclude treaties

Every state possesses capacity to conclude treaties.

Article 7

Full powers

1. A person is considered as representing a state for the purpose of adopting or authenticating the text of a treaty or for the purpose of expressing the consent of the state to be bound by a treaty if:

(a) he produces appropriate full powers; or

(b) it appears from the practice of the states concerned or from other circumstances that their intention was to consider that person as representing the state for such purposes and to dispense with full powers.

2. In virtue of their functions and without having to produce full powers, the following are considered as representing their state:

(a) Heads of State, Heads of Government and Ministers for Foreign Affairs, for the purpose of performing all acts relating to the conclusion of a treaty;

(b) heads of diplomatic missions, for the purpose of adopting the text of a treaty between the accrediting state and the state to which they are accredited;

(c) representatives accredited by states to an international conference or to an international organization or one of its organs, for the purpose of adopting the text of a treaty in that conference, organization or organ.

Article 8

Subsequent confirmation of an act
performed without authorization

An act relating to the conclusion of a treaty performed by a person who cannot be considered under Article 7 as authorized to represent a state for that purpose is without legal effect unless afterwards confirmed by that state.

Article 9

Adoption of the text

1. The adoption of the text of a treaty takes place by the consent of all the states participating in its drawing up except as provided in paragraph 2.

2. The adoption of the text of a treaty at an international conference takes place by the vote of two-thirds of the states present and voting, unless by the same majority they shall decide to apply a different rule.

Article 10

Authentication of the text

The text of a treaty is established as authentic and definitive:

(a) by such procedure as may be provided for in the text or agreed upon by the states participating in its drawing up; or

(b) failing such procedure, by the signature, signature *ad referendum* or initialling by the representatives of those states of the text of the treaty or of the Final Act of a conference incorporating the text.

Article 11

Means of expressing consent to be bound by a treaty

The consent of a state to be bound by a treaty may be expressed by signature, exchange of instruments constituting a treaty, ratification, acceptance, approval or accession, or by any other means if so agreed.

Article 12

Consent to be bound by a treaty expressed by signature

1. The consent of a state to be bound by a treaty is expressed by the signature of its representative when:

(a) the treaty provides that signature shall have that effect;

(b) it is otherwise established that the negotiating states were agreed that signature should have that effect; or

(c) the intention of the state to give that effect to the signature appears from the full powers of its representative or was expressed during the negotiation.

2. For the purposes of paragraph 1:

(a) the initialling of a text constitutes a signature of the treaty when it is established that the negotiating states so agreed;

(b) the signature *ad referendum* of a treaty by a representative, if confirmed by his state, constitutes a full signature of the treaty.

Article 13

Consent to be bound by a treaty expressed by an exchange of instruments constituting a treaty

The consent of states to be bound by a treaty constituted by instruments exchanged between them is expressed by that exchange when:

(a) the instruments provide that their exchange shall have that effect; or

(b) it is otherwise established that those states were agreed that the exchange of instruments should have that effect.

Article 14

Consent to be bound by a treaty expressed by ratification, acceptance or approval

1. The consent of a state to be bound by a treaty is expressed by ratification when:

(a) the treaty provides for such consent to be expressed by means of ratification;

(b) it is otherwise established that the negotiating states were agreed that ratification should be required;

(c) the representative of the state has signed the treaty subject to ratification; or

(d) the intention of the state to sign the treaty subject to ratification appears from the full powers of its representative or was expressed during the negotiation.

2. The consent of a state to be bound by a treaty is expressed by acceptance or approval under conditions similar to those which apply to ratification.

Article 15

Consent to be bound by a treaty expressed by accession

The consent of a state to be bound by a treaty is expressed by accession when:

(a) the treaty provides that such consent may be expressed by that state by means of accession; or

(b) it is otherwise established that the negotiating states were agreed that such consent may be expressed by that state by means of accession; or

(c) all the parties have subsequently agreed that such consent may be expressed by that state by means of accession.

Article 16

Exchange or deposit of instruments of ratification,
acceptance, approval or accession

Unless the treaty otherwise provides, instruments of ratification, acceptance, approval or accession establish the consent of a state to be bound by a treaty upon:

(a) their exchange between the contracting states;

(b) their deposit with the depositary; or

(c) their notification to the contracting states or to the depositary, if so agreed.

Article 17

Consent to be bound by part of a treaty and choice of differing provisions

1. Without prejudice to Articles 19 to 23, the consent of a state to be bound by part of a treaty is effective only if the treaty so permits or the other contracting states so agree.

2. The consent of a state to be bound by a treaty which permits a choice between differing provisions is effective only if it is made clear to which of the provisions the consent relates.

Article 18

Obligation not to defeat the object and purpose of a
treaty prior to its entry into force

A state is obliged to refrain from acts which would defeat the object and purpose of a treaty when:

(a) it has signed the treaty or has exchanged instruments constituting the treaty subject to ratification, acceptance or approval until it shall have made its intention clear not to become a party to the treaty; or

(b) it has expressed its consent to be bound by the treaty, pending the entry into force of the treaty and provided that such entry into force is not unduly delayed.

SECTION 2. RESERVATIONS

Article 19

Formulation of reservations

A state may, when signing, ratifying, accepting, approving or acceding to a treaty, formulate a reservation unless:

(a) the reservation is prohibited by the treaty;

(b) the treaty provides that only specified reservations, which do not include the reservation in question, may be made; or

(c) in cases not falling under sub-paragraphs (a) and (b), the reservation is incompatible with the object and purpose of the treaty.

Article 20

Acceptance of and objection to reservations

1. A reservation expressly authorized by a treaty does not require any subsequent acceptance by the other contracting states unless the treaty so provides.

2. When it appears from the limited number of the negotiating states and the object and purpose of a treaty that the application of the treaty in its entirety between all the parties is an essential condition of the consent of each one to be bound by the treaty, a reservation requires acceptance by all the parties.

3. When a treaty is a constituent instrument of an international organization and unless it otherwise provides, a reservation requires the acceptance of the competent organ of that organization.

4. In cases not falling under the preceding paragraphs and unless the treaty otherwise provides:

(a) acceptance by another contracting state of a reservation constitutes the reserving state a party to the treaty in relation to that other state if or when the treaty is in force for those states;

(b) an objection by another contracting state to a reservation does not preclude the entry into force of the treaty as between the objecting and reserving states unless a contrary intention is definitely expressed by the objecting state;

(c) an act expressing a state's consent to be bound by the treaty and containing a reservation is effective as soon as at least one other contracting state has accepted the reservation.

5. For the purposes of paragraphs 2 and 4 and unless the treaty otherwise provides, a reservation is considered to have been accepted by a state if it shall have raised no objection to the reservation by the end of a period of twelve months after it was notified of the reservation or by the date on which it expressed its consent to be bound by the treaty, whichever is later.

Article 21

Legal effects of reservations and of objections to reservations

1. A reservation established with regard to another party in accordance with Articles 19, 20 and 23:

(a) modifies for the reserving state in its relations with that other party the provisions of the treaty to which the reservation relates to the extent of the reservation; and

(b) modifies those provisions to the same extent for that other party in its relations with the reserving state.

2. The reservation does not modify the provisions of the treaty for the other parties to the treaty *inter se*.

3. When a state objecting to a reservation has not opposed the entry into force of the treaty between itself and the reserving state, the provisions to which the reservation relates do not apply as between the two states to the extent of the reservation.

Article 22

Withdrawal of reservations and of objections to reservations

1. Unless the treaty otherwise provides, a reservation may be withdrawn at any time and the consent of a state which has accepted the reservation is not required for its withdrawal.

2. Unless the treaty otherwise provides, an objection to a reservation may be withdrawn at any time.

3. Unless the treaty otherwise provides, or it is otherwise agreed:

(a) the withdrawal of a reservation becomes operative in relation to another contracting state only when notice of it has been received by that state;

(b) the withdrawal of an objection to a reservation becomes operative only when notice of it has been received by the state which formulated the reservation.

Article 23

Procedure regarding reservations

1. A reservation, an express acceptance of a reservation and an objection to a reservation must be formulated in writing and communicated to the contracting states and other states entitled to become parties to the treaty.

2. If formulated when signing the treaty subject to ratification, acceptance or approval, a reservation must be formally confirmed by the reserving state when expressing its consent to be bound by the treaty. In such a case the reservation shall be considered as having been made on the date of its confirmation.

3. An express acceptance of, or an objection to, a reservation made previously to confirmation of the reservation does not itself require confirmation.

4. The withdrawal of a reservation or of an objection to a reservation must be formulated in writing.

SECTION 3. ENTRY INTO FORCE AND PROVISIONAL APPLICATION OF TREATIES

Article 24

Entry into force

1. A treaty enters into force in such manner and upon such date as it may provide or as the negotiating states may agree.

2. Failing any such provision or agreement, a treaty enters into force as soon as consent to be bound by the treaty has been established for all the negotiating states.

3. When the consent of a state to be bound by a treaty is established on a date after the treaty has come into force, the treaty enters into force for that state on that date, unless the treaty otherwise provides.

4. The provisions of a treaty regulating the authentication of its text, the establishment of the consent of states to be bound by the treaty, the manner or date of its entry into force, reservations, the functions of the depositary and other matters arising necessarily before the entry into force of the treaty apply from the time of the adoption of its text.

Article 25

Provisional application

1. A treaty or a part of a treaty is applied provisionally pending its entry into force if:

(a) the treaty itself so provides; or

(b) the negotiating states have in some other manner so agreed.

2. Unless the treaty otherwise provides or the negotiating states have otherwise agreed, the provisional application of a treaty or a part of a treaty with respect to a state shall be

terminated if that state notifies the other states between which the treaty is being applied provisionally of its intention not to become a party to the treaty.

PART III
OBSERVANCE, APPLICATION AND INTERPRETATION OF TREATIES

SECTION 1. OBSERVANCE OF TREATIES

Article 26

Pacta sunt servanda

Every treaty in force is binding upon the parties to it and must be performed by them in good faith.

Article 27

Internal law and observance of treaties

A party may not invoke the provisions of its internal law as justification for its failure to perform a treaty. This rule is without prejudice to Article 46.

SECTION 2. APPLICATION OF TREATIES

Article 28

Non-retroactivity of treaties

Unless a different intention appears from the treaty or is otherwise established, its provisions do not bind a party in relation to any act or fact which took place or any situation which ceased to exist before the date of the entry into force of the treaty with respect to that party.

Article 29

Territorial scope of treaties

Unless a different intention appears from the treaty or is otherwise established, a treaty is binding upon each party in respect of its entire territory.

Article 30

Application of successive treaties relating to the same subject-matter

1. Subject to Article 103 of the Charter of the United Nations, the rights and obligations of states parties to successive treaties relating to the same subject-matter shall be determined in accordance with the following paragraphs.

2. When a treaty specifies that it is subject to, or that it is not to be considered as incompatible with, an earlier or later treaty, the provisions of that other treaty prevail.

3. When all the parties to the earlier treaty are parties also to the later treaty but the earlier treaty is not terminated or suspended in operation under Article 59, the earlier treaty applies only to the extent that its provisions are compatible with those of the later treaty.

4. When the parties to the later treaty do not include all the parties to the earlier one:

(a) as between states parties to both treaties the same rule applies as in paragraph 3;

(b) as between a state party to both treaties and a state party to only one of the treaties, the treaty to which both states are parties governs their mutual rights and obligations.

5. Paragraph 4 is without prejudice to Article 41, or to any question of the termination or suspension of the operation of a treaty under Article 60 or to any question of responsibility which may arise for a state from the conclusion or application of a treaty the provisions of which are incompatible with its obligations towards another state under another treaty.

SECTION 3. INTERPRETATION OF TREATIES

Article 31

General rule of interpretation

1. A treaty shall be interpreted in good faith in accordance with the ordinary meaning to be given to the terms of the treaty in their context and in the light of its object and purpose.

2. The context for the purpose of the interpretation of a treaty shall comprise, in addition to the text, including its preamble and annexes:

(a) any agreement relating to the treaty which was made between all the parties in connexion with the conclusion of the treaty;

(b) any instrument which was made by one or more parties in connexion with the conclusion of the treaty and accepted by the other parties as an instrument related to the treaty.

3. There shall be taken into account, together with the context:

(a) any subsequent agreement between the parties regarding the interpretation of the treaty or the application of its provisions;

(b) any subsequent practice in the application of the treaty which establishes the agreement of the parties regarding its interpretation;

(c) any relevant rules of international law applicable in the relations between the parties.

4. A special meaning shall be given to a term if it is established that the parties so intended.

Article 32

Supplementary means of interpretation

Recourse may be had to supplementary means of interpretation, including the preparatory work of the treaty and the circumstances of its conclusion, in order to confirm the meaning resulting from the application of Article 31, or to determine the meaning when the interpretation according to Article 31:

(a) leaves the meaning ambiguous or obscure; or

(b) leads to a result which is manifestly absurd or unreasonable.

Article 33

Interpretation of treaties authenticated in two or more languages

1. When a treaty has been authenticated in two or more languages, the text is equally authoritative in each language, unless the treaty provides or the parties agree that, in case of divergence, a particular text shall prevail.

2. A version of the treaty in a language other than one of those in which the text was authenticated shall be considered an authentic text only if the treaty so provides or the parties so agree.

3. The terms of the treaty are presumed to have the same meaning in each authentic text.

4. Except where a particular text prevails in accordance with paragraph 1, when a comparison of the authentic texts discloses a difference of meaning which the application of Articles 31 and 32 does not remove, the meaning which best reconciles the texts, having regard to the object and purpose of the treaty, shall be adopted.

SECTION 4. TREATIES AND THIRD STATES

Article 34

General rule regarding third states

A treaty does not create either obligations or rights for a third state without its consent.

Article 35

Treaties providing for obligations for third states

An obligation arises for a third state from a provision of a treaty if the parties to the treaty intend the provision to be the means of establishing the obligation and the third state expressly accepts that obligation in writing.

Article 36

Treaties providing for rights for third states

1. A right arises for a third state from a provision of a treaty if the parties to the treaty intend the provision to accord that right either to the third state, or to a group of states to which it belongs, or to all states, and the third state assents thereto. Its assent shall be presumed so long as the contrary is not indicated, unless the treaty otherwise provides.

2. A state exercising a right in accordance with paragraph 1 shall comply with the conditions for its exercise provided for in the treaty or established in conformity with the treaty.

Article 37

Revocation or modification of obligations or rights of third states

1. When an obligation has arisen for a third state in conformity with Article 35, the obligation may be revoked or modified only with the consent of the parties to the treaty and of the third state, unless it is established that they had otherwise agreed.

2. When a right has arisen for a third state in conformity with Article 36, the right may not be revoked or modified by the parties if it is established that the right was intended not to be revocable or subject to modification without the consent of the third state.

Article 38

Rules in a treaty becoming binding on third states through international custom

Nothing in Articles 34 to 37 precludes a rule set forth in a treaty from becoming binding upon a third state as a customary rule of international law, recognized as such.

PART IV
AMENDMENT AND MODIFICATION OF TREATIES

Article 39

General rule regarding the
amendment of treaties

A treaty may be amended by agreement between the parties. The rules laid down in Part II apply to such an agreement except in so far as the treaty may otherwise provide.

Article 40

Amendment of multilateral treaties

1. Unless the treaty otherwise provides, the amendment of multilateral treaties shall be governed by the following paragraphs.

2. Any proposal to amend a multilateral treaty as between all the parties must be notified to all the contracting states, each one of which shall have the right to take part in:

(a) the decision as to the action to be taken in regard to such proposal;

(b) the negotiation and conclusion of any agreement for the amendment of the treaty.

3. Every state entitled to become a party to the treaty shall also be entitled to become a party to the treaty as amended.

4. The amending agreement does not bind any state already a party to the treaty which does not become a party to the amending agreement; Article 30, paragraph 4(b).

5. Any state which becomes a party to the treaty after the entry into force of the amending agreement shall, failing an expression of a different intention by that state:

(a) be considered as a party to the treaty as amended, and

(b) be considered as a party to the unamended treaty in relation to any party to the treaty not bound by the amending agreement.

Article 41

Agreements to modify multilateral treaties
between certain of the parties only

1. Two or more of the parties to a multilateral treaty may conclude an agreement to modify the treaty as between themselves alone if:

(a) the possibility of such a modification is provided for by the treaty; or

(b) the modification in question is not prohibited by the treaty and:

(i) does not affect the enjoyment by the other parties of their rights under the treaty or the performance of their obligations;

(ii) does not relate to a provision, derogation from which is incompatible with the effective execution of the object and purpose of the treaty as a whole.

2. Unless in a case falling under paragraph 1(a) the treaty otherwise provides, the parties in question shall notify the other parties of their intention to conclude the agreement and of the modification to the treaty for which it provides.

PART V
INVALIDITY, TERMINATION AND SUSPENSION OF
THE OPERATION OF TREATIES

SECTION 1. GENERAL PROVISIONS

Article 42

Validity and continuance in force of treaties

1. The validity of a treaty or of the consent of a state to be bound by a treaty may be impeached only through the application of the present Convention.

2. The termination of a treaty, its denunciation or the withdrawal of a party, may take place only as a result of the application of the provisions of the treaty or of the present Convention. The same rule applies to suspension of the operation of a treaty.

Article 43

Obligations imposed by international law
independently of a treaty

The invalidity, termination or denunciation of a treaty, the withdrawal of a party from it, or the suspension of its operation, as a result of the application of the present Convention or of the provisions of the treaty, shall not in any way impair the duty of any state to fulfil any obligation embodied in the treaty to which it would be subject under international law independently of the treaty.

Article 44

Separability of treaty provisions

1. A right of a party, provided for in a treaty or arising under Article 56, to denounce, withdraw from or suspend the operation of the treaty may be exercised only with respect to the whole treaty unless the treaty otherwise provides or the parties otherwise agree.

2. A ground for invalidating, terminating, withdrawing from or suspending the operation of a treaty recognized in the present Convention may be invoked only with respect to the whole treaty except as provided in the following paragraphs or in Article 60.

3. If the ground relates solely to particular clauses, it may be invoked only with respect to those clauses where:

(a) the said clauses are separable from the remainder of the treaty with regard to their application;

(b) it appears from the treaty or is otherwise established that acceptance of those clauses was not an essential basis of the consent of the other party or parties to be bound by the treaty as a whole; and

(c) continued performance of the remainder of the treaty would not be unjust.

4. In cases falling under Articles 49 and 50 the state entitled to invoke the fraud or corruption may do so with respect either to the whole treaty or, subject to paragraph 3, to the particular clauses alone.

5. In cases falling under Articles 51, 52 and 53, no separation of the provisions of the treaty is permitted.

Article 45

Loss of a right to invoke a ground for invalidating,
terminating, withdrawing from or suspending the operation of a treaty

A state may no longer invoke a ground for invalidating, terminating, withdrawing from or suspending the operation of a treaty under Articles 46 to 50 or Articles 60 to 62, if, after becoming aware of the facts:

(a) it shall have expressly agreed that the treaty is valid or remains in force or continues in operation, as the case may be; or

(b) it must by reason of its conduct be considered as having acquiesced in the validity of the treaty or in its maintenance in force or in operation, as the case may be.

SECTION 2. INVALIDITY OF TREATIES

Article 46

Provisions of internal law regarding
competence to conclude treaties

1. A state may not invoke the fact that its consent to be bound by a treaty has been expressed in violation of a provision of its internal law regarding competence to conclude treaties as invalidating its consent unless that violation was manifest and concerned a rule of its internal law of fundamental importance.

2. A violation is manifest if it would be objectively evident to any state conducting itself in the matter in accordance with normal practice and in good faith.

Article 47

Specific restrictions on authority to
express the consent of a state

If the authority of a representative to express the consent of a state to be bound by a particular treaty has been made subject to a specific restriction, his omission to observe that restriction may not be invoked as invalidating the consent expressed by him unless the restriction was notified to the other negotiating states prior to his expressing such consent.

Article 48

Error

1. A state may invoke an error in a treaty as invalidating its consent to be bound by the treaty if the error relates to a fact or situation which was assumed by that state to exist at the time when the treaty was concluded and formed an essential basis of its consent to be bound by the treaty.

2. Paragraph 1 shall not apply if the state in question contributed by its own conduct to the error or if the circumstances were such as to put that state on notice of a possible error.

3. An error relating only to the wording of the text of a treaty does not affect its validity; Article 79 then applies.

Article 49

Fraud

If a state has been induced to conclude a treaty by the fraudulent conduct of another negotiating state, the state may invoke the fraud as invalidating its consent to be bound by the treaty.

Article 50

Corruption of a representative of a state

If the expression of a state's consent to be bound by a treaty has been procured through the corruption of its representative directly or indirectly by another negotiating state, the state may invoke such corruption as invalidating its consent to be bound by the treaty.

Article 51

Coercion of a representative of a state

The expression of a state's consent to be bound by a treaty which has been procured by the coercion of its representative through acts or threats directed against him shall be without any legal effect.

Article 52

Coercion of a state by the threat or use of force

A treaty is void if its conclusion has been procured by the threat or use of force in violation of the principles of international law embodied in the Charter of the United Nations.

Article 53

Treaties conflicting with a peremptory norm of general international law (jus cogens)

A treaty is void if, at the time of its conclusion, it conflicts with a peremptory norm of general international law. For the purposes of the present Convention, a peremptory norm of general international law is a norm accepted and recognized by the international community of states as a whole as a norm from which no derogation is permitted and which can be modified only by a subsequent norm of general international law having the same character.

SECTION 3. TERMINATION AND SUSPENSION OF THE OPERATION OF TREATIES

Article 54

Termination of or withdrawal from a treaty under its provisions or by consent of the parties

The termination of a treaty or the withdrawal of a party may take place:
    (a) in conformity with the provisions of the treaty, or
    (b) at any time by consent of all the parties after consultation with the other contracting states.

Article 55

*Reduction of the parties to a multilateral treaty below
the number necessary for its entry into force*

Unless the treaty otherwise provides, a multilateral treaty does not terminate by reason only of the fact that the number of the parties falls below the number necessary for its entry into force.

Article 56

*Denunciation of or withdrawal from a
treaty containing no provision regarding
termination, denunciation or withdrawal*

1. A treaty which contains no provision regarding its termination and which does not provide for denunciation or withdrawal is not subject to denunciation or withdrawal unless:

(a) it is established that the parties intended to admit the possibility of denunciation or withdrawal; or

(b) a right of denunciation or withdrawal may be implied by the nature of the treaty.

2. A party shall give not less than twelve months' notice of its intention to denounce or withdraw from a treaty under paragraph 1.

Article 57

*Suspension of the operation of a treaty under its
provisions or by consent of the parties*

The operation of a treaty in regard to all the parties or to a particular party may be suspended:

(a) in conformity with the provisions of the treaty; or

(b) at any time by consent of all the parties after consultation with the other contracting states.

Article 58

*Suspension of the operation of a multilateral treaty by
agreement between certain of the parties only*

1. Two or more parties to a multilateral treaty may conclude an agreement to suspend the operation of provisions of the treaty, temporarily and as between themselves alone, if:

(a) the possibility of such a suspension is provided for by the treaty; or

(b) the suspension in question is not prohibited by the treaty and:

(i) does not affect the enjoyment by the other parties of their rights under the treaty or the performance of their obligations;

(ii) is not incompatible with the object and purpose of the treaty.

2. Unless in a case falling under paragraph 1(a) the treaty otherwise provides, the parties in question shall notify the other parties of their intention to conclude the agreement and of those provisions of the treaty the operation of which they intend to suspend.

Article 59

Termination or suspension of the operation of a treaty implied
by conclusion of a later treaty

1. A treaty shall be considered as terminated if all the parties to it conclude a later treaty relating to the same subject-matter and:

(a) it appears from the later treaty or is otherwise established that the parties intended that the matter should be governed by that treaty; or

(b) the provisions of the later treaty are so far incompatible with those of the earlier one that the two treaties are not capable of being applied at the same time.

2. The earlier treaty shall be considered as only suspended in operation if it appears from the later treaty or is otherwise established that such was the intention of the parties.

Article 60

Termination or suspension of the operation of a treaty as a consequence of its breach

1. A material breach of a bilateral treaty by one of the parties entitles the other to invoke the breach as a ground for terminating the treaty or suspending its operation in whole or in part.

2. A material breach of a multilateral treaty by one of the parties entitles:

(a) the other parties by unanimous agreement to suspend the operation of the treaty in whole or in part or to terminate it either:

(i) in the relations between themselves and the defaulting state; or

(ii) as between all the parties;

(b) a party specially affected by the breach to invoke it as a ground for suspending the operation of the treaty in whole or in part in the relations between itself and the defaulting state;

(c) any party other than the defaulting state to invoke the breach as a ground for suspending the operation of the treaty in whole or in part with respect to itself if the treaty is of such a character that a material breach of its provisions by one party radically changes the position of every party with respect to the further performance of its obligations under the treaty.

3. A material breach of a treaty, for the purposes of this article, consists in:

(a) a repudiation of the treaty not sanctioned by the present Convention; or

(b) the violation of a provision essential to the accomplishment of the object or purpose of the treaty.

4. The foregoing paragraphs are without prejudice to any provision in the treaty applicable in the event of a breach.

5. Paragraphs 1 to 3 do not apply to provisions relating to the protection of the human person contained in treaties of a humanitarian character in particular to provisions prohibiting any form of reprisals against persons protected by such treaties.

Article 61

Supervening impossibility of performance

1. A party may invoke the impossibility of performing a treaty as a ground for terminating or withdrawing from it if the impossibility results from the permanent disappearance or

destruction of an object indispensable for the execution of the treaty. If the impossibility is temporary, it may be invoked only as a ground for suspending the operation of the treaty.

2. Impossibility of performance may not be invoked by a party as a ground for terminating, withdrawing from or suspending the operation of a treaty if the impossibility is the result of a breach by that party either of an obligation under the treaty or of any other international obligation owed to any other party to the treaty.

Article 62

Fundamental change of circumstances

1. A fundamental change of circumstances which has occurred with regard to those existing at the time of the conclusion of a treaty, and which was not foreseen by the parties, may not be invoked as a ground for terminating or withdrawing from the treaty unless:

(a) the existence of those circumstances constituted an essential basis of the consent of the parties to be bound by the treaty; and

(b) the effect of the change is radically to transform the extent of obligations still to be performed under the treaty.

2. A fundamental change of circumstances may not be invoked as a ground for terminating or withdrawing from a treaty:

(a) if the treaty establishes a boundary; or

(b) if the fundamental change is the result of a breach by the party invoking it either of an obligation under the treaty or of any other international obligation owed to any other party to the treaty.

3. If, under the foregoing paragraphs, a party may invoke a fundamental change of circumstances as a ground for terminating or withdrawing from a treaty it may also invoke the change as a ground for suspending the operation of the treaty.

Article 63

Severance of diplomatic or consular relations

The severance of diplomatic or consular relations between parties to a treaty does not affect the legal relations established between them by the treaty except in so far as the existence of diplomatic or consular relations is indispensable for the application of the treaty.

Article 64

Emergence of a new peremptory norm of general international law (jus cogens)

If a new peremptory norm of general international law emerges, any existing treaty which is in conflict with that norm becomes void and terminates.

• • •

Article 69

Consequences of the invalidity of a treaty

1. A treaty the invalidity of which is established under the present Convention is void. The provisions of a void treaty have no legal force.

2. If acts have nevertheless been performed in reliance on such a treaty:

(a) each party may require any other party to establish as far as possible in their mutual relations the position that would have existed if the acts had not been performed;

(b) acts performed in good faith before the invalidity was invoked are not rendered unlawful by reason only of the invalidity of the treaty.

3. In cases falling under Articles 49, 50, 51 or 52, paragraph 2 does not apply with respect to the party to which the fraud, the act of corruption or the coercion is imputable.

4. In the case of the invalidity of a particular state's consent to be bound by a multilateral treaty, the foregoing rules apply in the relations between that state and the parties to the treaty.

Article 70

Consequences of the termination of a treaty

1. Unless the treaty otherwise provides or the parties otherwise agree, the termination of a treaty under its provisions or in accordance with the present Convention:

(a) releases the parties from any obligation further to perform the treaty;

(b) does not affect any right, obligation or legal situation of the parties created through the execution of the treaty prior to its termination.

2. If a state denounces or withdraws from a multilateral treaty, paragraph 1 applies in the relations between that state and each of the other parties to the treaty from the date when such denunciation or withdrawal takes effect.

Article 71

Consequences of the invalidity of a treaty which conflicts with a peremptory norm of general international law

1. In the case of a treaty which is void under Article 53 the parties shall:

(a) eliminate as far as possible the consequences of any act performed in reliance on any provision which conflicts with the peremptory norm of general international law; and

(b) bring their mutual relations into conformity with the peremptory norm of general international law.

2. In the case of a treaty which becomes void and terminates under Article 64, the termination of the treaty:

(a) releases the parties from any obligation further to perform the treaty;

(b) does not affect any right, obligation or legal situation of the parties created through the execution of the treaty prior to its termination; provided that those rights, obligations or situations may thereafter be maintained only to the extent that their maintenance is not in itself in conflict with the new peremptory norm of general international law.

Article 72

Consequences of the suspension of the operation of a treaty

1. Unless the treaty otherwise provides or the parties otherwise agree, the suspension of the operation of a treaty under its provisions or in accordance with the present Convention:

(a) releases the parties between which the operation of the treaty is suspended from the obligation to perform the treaty in their mutual relations during the period of the suspension;

(b) does not otherwise affect the legal relations between the parties established by the treaty.

2. During the period of the suspension the parties shall refrain from acts tending to obstruct the resumption of the operation of the treaty.

PART VI
MISCELLANEOUS PROVISIONS

Article 73

Cases of state succession, state responsibility and outbreaks of hostilities
The provisions of the present Convention shall not prejudge any question that may arise in regard to a treaty from a succession of states or from the international responsibility of a state or from the outbreak of hostilities between states.

• • •

PART VII
DEPOSITARIES, NOTIFICATIONS, CORRECTIONS AND REGISTRATION

• • •

Article 80

Registration and publication of treaties
1. Treaties shall, after their entry into force, be transmitted to the Secretariat of the United Nations for registration or filing and recording, as the case may be, and for publication.

2. The designation of a depositary shall constitute authorization for it to perform the acts specified in the preceding paragraph.

V
Vienna Convention on Diplomatic Relations
(1961) 500 U.N.T.S. 95, Can. T.S. 1966 No. 29, in force 1964, in force for Canada 1966

The States Parties to the Present Convention,

Recalling that people of all nations from ancient times have recognized the status of diplomatic agents, ...

Realizing that the purpose of such privileges and immunities is not to benefit individuals but to ensure the efficient performance of the functions of diplomatic missions as representing states,

Affirming that the rules of customary international law should continue to govern questions not expressly regulated by the provisions of the present Convention,

Have agreed as follows:

Article 1

For the purpose of the present Convention, the following expressions shall have the meanings hereunder assigned to them:

(a) the "head of the mission" is the person charged by the sending state with the duty of acting in that capacity;

(b) the "members of the mission" are the head of the mission and the members of the staff of the mission;

(c) the "members of the staff of the mission" are the members of the diplomatic staff, of the administrative and technical staff and of the service staff of the mission;

(d) the "members of the diplomatic staff" are the members of the staff of the mission having diplomatic rank;

(e) a "diplomatic agent" is the head of the mission or a member of the diplomatic staff of the mission;

(f) the "members of the administrative and technical staff" are the members of the staff of the mission employed in the administrative and technical service of the mission;

(g) the "members of the service staff" are the members of the staff of the mission in the domestic service of the mission;

(h) a "private servant" is a person who is in the domestic service of a member of the mission and who is not an employee of the sending state;

(i) the "premises of the mission" are the buildings or parts of buildings and the land ancillary thereto, irrespective of ownership, used for the purposes of the mission including the residence of the head of the mission.

Article 2

The establishment of diplomatic relations between states, and of permanent diplomatic missions, takes place by mutual consent.

Article 3

1. The functions of a diplomatic mission consist *inter alia* in:

(a) representing the sending state in the receiving state;

(b) protecting in the receiving state the interests of the sending state and of its nationals, within the limits permitted by international law;

(c) negotiating with the government of the receiving state;

(d) ascertaining by all lawful means conditions and developments in the receiving state, and reporting thereon to the government of the sending state;

(e) promoting friendly relations between the sending state and the receiving state, and developing their economic, cultural and scientific relations.

• • •

Article 9

1. The receiving State may at any time and without having to explain its decision, notify the sending State that the head of the mission or any member of the diplomatic staff of the mission is *persona non grata* or that any other member of the staff of the mission is not acceptable. In any such case, the sending State shall, as appropriate, either recall the person concerned or terminate his functions with the mission. A person may be declared *non grata* or not acceptable before arriving in the territory of the receiving State.

2. If the sending State refuses or fails within a reasonable period to carry out its obligations under paragraph 1 of this Article, the receiving State may refuse to recognize the person concerned as a member of the mission.

• • •

Article 22

1. The premises of the mission shall be inviolable. The agents of the receiving state may not enter them, except with the consent of the head of the mission.

2. The receiving state is under a special duty to take all appropriate steps to protect the premises of the mission against any intrusion or damage and to prevent any disturbance of the peace of the mission or impairment of its dignity.

3. The premises of the mission, their furnishings and other property thereon and the means of transport of the mission shall be immune from search, requisition, attachment or execution.

Article 23

1. The sending state and the head of the mission shall be exempt from all national, regional or municipal dues and taxes in respect of the premises of the mission, whether owned or leased, other than such as represent payment for specific services rendered. …

Article 24

The archives and documents of the mission shall be inviolable at any time and wherever they may be.

Article 25

The receiving state shall accord full facilities for the performance of the functions of the mission.

Article 26

Subject to its laws and regulations concerning zones entry into which is prohibited or regulated for reasons of national security, the receiving state shall ensure to all members of the mission freedom of movement and travel in its territory.

Article 27

1. The receiving state shall permit and protect free communication on the part of the mission for all official purposes. In communicating with the government and the other missions and consulates of the sending state, wherever situated, the mission may employ all appropriate means, including diplomatic couriers and messages in code or cipher. However, the mission may install and use a wireless transmitter only with the consent of the receiving state.

2. The official correspondence of the mission shall be inviolable. Official correspondence means all correspondence relating to the mission and its functions.

3. The diplomatic bag shall not be opened or detained.

4. The packages constituting the diplomatic bag must bear visible external marks of their character and may contain only diplomatic documents or articles intended for official use.

5. The diplomatic courier, who shall be provided with an official document indicating his status and the number of packages constituting the diplomatic bag, shall be protected by the receiving state in the performance of his functions. He shall enjoy personal inviolability and shall not be liable to any form of arrest or detention.

Article 28

The fees and charges levied by the mission in the course of its official duties shall be exempt from all dues and taxes.

Article 29

The person of a diplomatic agent shall be inviolable. He shall not be liable to any form of arrest or detention. The receiving state shall treat him with due respect and shall take all appropriate steps to prevent any attack on his person, freedom or dignity.

Article 30

1. The private residence of a diplomatic agent shall enjoy the same inviolability and protection as the premises of the mission.

2. His papers, correspondence and, except as provided in paragraph 3 of Article 31, his property, shall likewise enjoy inviolability.

Article 31

1. A diplomatic agent shall enjoy immunity from the criminal jurisdiction of the receiving State. He shall also enjoy immunity from its civil and administrative jurisdiction, except in the case of:

(a) a real action relating to private immovable property situated in the territory of the receiving State, unless he holds it on behalf of the sending State for the purposes of the mission;

(b) an action relating to succession in which the diplomatic agent is involved as executor, administrator, heir or legatee as a private person and not on behalf of the sending State;

(c) an action relating to any professional or commercial activity exercised by the diplomatic agent in the receiving State outside his official functions.

2. A diplomatic agent is not obliged to give evidence as a witness.

3. No measures of execution may be taken in respect of a diplomatic agent except in the cases coming under sub-paragraphs (a), (b) and (c) of paragraph 1 of this Article, and provided that the measures concerned can be taken without infringing the inviolability of his person or of his residence.

4. The immunity of a diplomatic agent from the jurisdiction of the receiving State does not exempt him from the jurisdiction of the sending State.

Article 32

1. The immunity from jurisdiction of diplomatic agents and of persons enjoying immunity under Article 37 may be waived by the sending State.

2. Waiver must always be express.

3. The initiation of proceedings by a diplomatic agent or by a person enjoying immunity from jurisdiction under Article 37 shall preclude him from invoking immunity from jurisdiction in respect of any counterclaim directly connected with the principal claim.

4. Waiver of immunity from jurisdiction in respect of civil or administrative proceedings shall not be held to imply waiver of immunity in respect of the execution of the judgment, for which a separate waiver shall be necessary.

Article 33

1. Subject to the provisions of paragraph 3 of this Article, a diplomatic agent shall with respect to services rendered for the sending State be exempt from social security provisions which may be in force in the receiving State.

2. The exemption provided for in paragraph 1 of this Article shall also apply to private servants who are in the sole employ of a diplomatic agent, on conditions:

(a) that they are not nationals of or permanently resident in the receiving State; and

(b) that they are covered by the social security provisions which may be in force in the sending State or a third State.

3. A diplomatic agent who employs persons to whom the exemption provided for in paragraph 2 of this Article does not apply shall observe the obligations which the social security provisions of the receiving State impose upon employers.

4. The exemption provided for in paragraphs 1 and 2 of this Article shall not preclude voluntary participation in the social security system of the receiving State provided that such participation is permitted by that State.

5. The provisions of this Article shall not affect bilateral or multilateral agreements concerning social security concluded previously and shall not prevent the conclusion of such agreements in the future.

Article 34

A diplomatic agent shall be exempt from all dues and taxes, personal or real, national, regional or municipal, except:

(a) indirect taxes of a kind which are normally incorporated in the price of goods or services;

(b) dues and taxes on private immovable property situated in the territory of the receiving State, unless he holds it on behalf of the sending State for the purposes of the mission;

(c) estate, succession or inheritance duties levied by the receiving State, subject to the provisions of paragraph 4 of Article 39;

(d) dues and taxes on private income having its source in the receiving State and capital taxes on investments made in commercial undertakings in the receiving State;

(e) charges levied for specific services rendered;

(f) registration, court or record fees, mortgage dues and stamp duty, with respect to immovable property, subject to the provisions of Article 23.

Article 35

The receiving State shall exempt diplomatic agents from all personal services, from all public service of any kind whatsoever, and from military obligations such as those connected with requisitioning, military contributions and billeting.

Article 36

1. The receiving State shall, in accordance with such laws and regulations as it may adopt, permit entry of and grant exemption from all customs duties, taxes, and related charges other than charges for storage, cartage and similar services, on:

(a) articles for the official use of the mission;

(b) articles for the personal use of a diplomatic agent or members of his family forming part of his household, including articles intended for his establishment.

2. The personal baggage of a diplomatic agent shall be exempt from inspection, unless there are serious grounds for presuming that it contains articles not covered by the exemptions mentioned in paragraph 1 of this article, or articles the import or export of which is prohibited by the law or controlled by the quarantine regulations of the receiving state. Such inspection shall be conducted only in the presence of the diplomatic agent or of his authorized representative.

Article 37

1. The members of the family of a diplomatic agent forming part of his household shall, if they are not nationals of the receiving state, enjoy the privileges and immunities specified in Articles 29 to 36.

2. Members of the administrative and technical staff of the mission, together with members of their families forming part of their respective households, shall, if they are not nationals of or permanently resident in the receiving state, enjoy the privileges and immunities specified in Articles 29 to 35, except that the immunity from civil and administrative jurisdiction of the receiving state specified in paragraph 1 of Article 31 shall not extend to acts performed outside the course of their duties. They shall also enjoy the privileges specified in Article 36, paragraph 1, in respect of articles imported at the time of first installation.

3. Members of the service staff of the mission who are not nationals of or permanently resident in the receiving state shall enjoy immunity in respect of acts performed in the course of their duties, exemption from dues and taxes on the emoluments they receive by reason of their employment and the exemption contained in Article 33.

4. Private servants of members of the mission shall, if they are not nationals of or permanently resident in the receiving state, be exempt from dues and taxes on the emoluments they receive by reason of their employment. In other respects, they may enjoy privileges and immunities only to the extent admitted by the receiving state. However, the receiving state must exercise its jurisdiction over those persons in such a manner as not to interfere unduly with the performance of the functions of the mission.

Article 38

1. Except insofar as additional privileges and immunities may be granted by the receiving state, a diplomatic agent who is a national of or permanently resident in that state shall enjoy only immunity from jurisdiction and inviolability, in respect of official acts performed in the exercise of his functions.

2. Other members of the staff of the mission and private servants who are nationals of or permanently resident in the receiving state shall enjoy privileges and immunities only to the extent admitted by the receiving state. However, the receiving state must exercise its jurisdiction over those persons in such a manner as not to interfere unduly with the performance of the functions of the mission.

Article 39

1. Every person entitled to privileges and immunities shall enjoy them from the moment he enters the territory of the receiving State on proceeding to take up his post or, if already in its territory, from the moment when his appointment is notified to the Ministry for Foreign Affairs or such other ministry as may be agreed.

2. When the functions of a person enjoying privileges and immunities have come to an end, such privileges and immunities shall normally cease at the moment when he leaves the country, or on expiry of a reasonable period in which to do so, but shall subsist until that time, even in case of armed conflict. However, with respect to acts performed by such a person in the exercise of his functions as a member of the mission, immunity shall continue to subsist.

...

Article 40

1. If a diplomatic agent passes through or is in the territory of a third State, which has granted him a passport visa if such visa was necessary, while proceeding to take up or to return to his post, or when returning to his own country, the third State shall accord him inviolability and such other immunities as may be required to ensure his transit or return. The same shall apply in the case of any members of his family enjoying privileges or immunities who are accompanying the diplomatic agent, or travelling separately to join him or to return to their country.

2. In circumstances similar to those specified in paragraph 1 of this Article, third States shall not hinder the passage of members of the administrative and technical or service staff of a mission, and of members of their families, through their territories.

3. Third States shall accord to official correspondence and other official communications in transit, including messages in code or cipher, the same freedom and protection as is accorded by the receiving State. They shall accord to diplomatic couriers, who have been granted a passport visa if such visa was necessary, and diplomatic bags in transit the same inviolability and protection as the receiving State is bound to accord.

4. The obligations of third States under paragraphs 1, 2 and 3 of this Article shall also apply to the persons mentioned respectively in those paragraphs, and to official communications and diplomatic bags, whose presence in the territory of the third State is due to *force majeure*.

Article 41

1. Without prejudice to their privileges and immunities, it is the duty of all persons enjoying such privileges and immunities to respect the laws and regulations of the receiving State. They also have a duty not to interfere in the internal affairs of that State.

2. All official business with the receiving State entrusted to the mission by the sending State shall be conducted with or through the Ministry for Foreign Affairs of the receiving State or such other ministry as may be agreed.

3. The premises of the mission must not be used in any manner incompatible with the functions of the mission as laid down in the present Convention or by other rules of general international law or by any special agreements in force between the sending and the receiving State.

Article 42

A diplomatic agent shall not in the receiving State practise for personal profit any professional or commercial activity.

Article 43

The function of a diplomatic agent comes to an end, *inter alia*:

(a) on notification by the sending State to the receiving State that the function of the diplomatic agent has come to an end;

(b) on notification by the receiving State to the sending State that, in accordance with paragraph 2 of Article 9, it refuses to recognize the diplomatic agent as a member of the mission.

Article 44

The receiving State must, even in case of armed conflict, grant facilities in order to enable persons enjoying privileges and immunities, other than nationals of the receiving State, and members of the families of such persons irrespective of their nationality, to leave at the earliest possible moment. It must, in particular, in case of need, place at their disposal the necessary means of transport for themselves and their property.

Article 45

If diplomatic relations are broken off between two States, or if a mission is permanently or temporarily recalled:

(a) the receiving State must, even in case of armed conflict, respect and protect the premises of the mission, together with its property and archives;

(b) the sending State may entrust the custody of the premises of the mission, together with its property and archives, to a third State acceptable to the receiving State;

(c) the sending State may entrust the protection of its interests and those of its nationals to a third State acceptable to the receiving State.

Article 46

A sending State may with the prior consent of a receiving State, and at the request of a third State not represented in the receiving State, undertake the temporary protection of the interests of the third State and of its nationals.

VI
Universal Declaration of Human Rights

UNGA Res. 217(III), UN GAOR, 3rd Sess., Supp. No. 13, at 71,
UN Doc. A/810 (1948), adopted by vote 48-0, with 8 abstentions

Preamble

Whereas recognition of the inherent dignity and of the equal and inalienable rights of all members of the human family is the foundation of freedom, justice and peace in the world.

Whereas disregard and contempt for human rights have resulted in barbarous acts which have outraged the conscience of mankind, and the advent of a world in which human beings shall enjoy freedom of speech and belief and freedom from fear and want has been proclaimed as the highest aspiration of the common people,

Whereas it is essential, if man is not to be compelled to have recourse, as a last resort, to rebellion against tyranny and oppression, that human rights should be protected by the rule of law,

Whereas it is essential to promote the development of friendly relations between nations,

Whereas the peoples of the United Nations have in the Charter reaffirmed their faith in fundamental human rights, in the dignity and worth of the human person and in the equal rights of men and women and have determined to promote social progress and better standards of life in larger freedom,

Whereas Member States have pledged themselves to achieve, in co-operation with the United Nations, the promotion of universal respect for and observance of human rights and fundamental freedoms,

Whereas a common understanding of these rights and freedoms is of the greatest importance for the full realization of this pledge,

Now, Therefore,

The General Assembly

Proclaims this Universal Declaration of Human Rights as a common standard of achievement for all peoples and all nations, to the end that every individual and every organ of society, keeping this Declaration constantly in mind, shall strive by teaching and education to promote respect for these rights and freedoms and by progressive measures, national and international, to secure their universal and effective recognition and observance, both among the peoples of Member States themselves and among the peoples of territories under their jurisdiction.

Article 1

All human beings are born free and equal in dignity and rights. They are endowed with reason and conscience and should act towards one another in a spirit of brotherhood.

Article 2

Everyone is entitled to all the rights and freedoms set forth in this Declaration, without distinction of any kind, such as race, colour, sex, language, religion, political or other opinion, national or social origin, property, birth or other status.

Furthermore, no distinction shall be made on the basis of the political, jurisdictional or international status of the country or territory to which a person belongs, whether it be independent, trust, non-self-governing or under any other limitation of sovereignty.

Article 3
Everyone has the right to life, liberty and the security of person.

Article 4
No one shall be held in slavery or servitude; slavery and the slave trade shall be prohibited in all their forms.

Article 5
No one shall be subjected to torture or to cruel, inhuman or degrading treatment or punishment.

Article 6
Everyone has the right to recognition everywhere as a person before the law.

Article 7
All are equal before the law and are entitled without any discrimination to equal protection of the law. All are entitled to equal protection against any discrimination in violation of this Declaration and against any incitement to such discrimination.

Article 8
Everyone has the right to an effective remedy by the competent national tribunals for acts violating the fundamental rights granted him by the constitution or by law.

Article 9
No one shall be subjected to arbitrary arrest, detention or exile.

Article 10
Everyone is entitled to full equality to a fair and public hearing by an independent and impartial tribunal, in the determination of his rights and obligations and of any criminal charge against him.

Article 11
1. Everyone charged with a penal offence has the right to be presumed innocent until proved guilty according to law in a public trial at which he has had all the guarantees necessary for his defence.

2. No one shall be held guilty of any penal offence on account of any act or omission which did not constitute a penal offence, under national or international law, at the time when it was committed. Nor shall a heavier penalty be imposed than the one that was applicable at the time the penal offence was committed.

Article 12
No one shall be subjected to arbitrary interference with his privacy, family, home or correspondence, nor to attacks upon his honour and reputation. Everyone has the right to the protection of the law against such interference or attacks.

Article 13
1. Everyone has the right to freedom of movement and residence within the borders of each State.
2. Everyone has the right to leave any country, including his own, and to return to his country.

Article 14
1. Everyone has the right to seek and to enjoy in other countries asylum from persecution.
2. This right may not be invoked in the case of prosecutions genuinely arising from non-political crimes or from acts contrary to the purposes and principles of the United Nations.

Article 15
1. Everyone has the right to a nationality.
2. No one shall be arbitrarily deprived of his nationality nor denied the right to change his nationality.

Article 16
1. Men and women of full age, without any limitation due to race, nationality or religion, have the right to marry and to found a family. They are entitled to equal rights as to marriage, during marriage and at its dissolution.
2. Marriage shall be entered into only with the free and full consent of the intending spouses.
3. The family is the natural and fundamental group unit of society and is entitled to protection by society and the State.

Article 17
1. Everyone has the right to own property alone as well as in association with others.
2. No one shall be arbitrarily deprived of his property.

Article 18
Everyone has the right to freedom of thought, conscience and religion; this right includes freedom to change his religion or belief, and freedom, either alone or in community with others and in public or private, to manifest his religion or belief in teaching, practice, worship and observance.

Article 19
Everyone has the right to freedom of opinion and expression; this right includes freedom to hold opinions without interference and to seek, receive and impart information and ideas through any media and regardless of frontiers.

Article 20

1. Everyone has the right to freedom of peaceful assembly and association.

2. No one may be compelled to belong to an association.

Article 21

1. Everyone has the right to take part in the government of his country, directly or through freely chosen representatives.

2. Everyone has the right of equal access to public service in his country.

3. The will of the people shall be the basis of the authority of government; this will shall be expressed in periodic and genuine elections which shall be by universal and equal suffrage and shall be held by secret vote or by equivalent free voting procedures.

Article 22

Everyone, as a member of society, has the right to social security and is entitled to realization, through national effort and international co-operation and in accordance with the organization and resources of each State, of the economic, social and cultural rights indispensable for his dignity and the free development of his personality.

Article 23

1. Everyone has the right to work, to free choice of employment, to just and favourable conditions of work and to protection against unemployment.

2. Everyone, without any discrimination, has the right to equal pay for equal work.

3. Everyone who works has the right to just and favourable remuneration ensuring for himself and his family an existence worthy of human dignity, and supplemented, if necessary, by other means of social protection.

4. Everyone has the right to form and to join trade unions for the protection of his interests.

Article 24

Everyone has the right to rest and leisure, including reasonable limitation of working hours and periodic holidays with pay.

Article 25

1. Everyone has the right to a standard of living adequate for the health and well-being of himself and of his family, including food, clothing, housing and medical care and necessary social services, and the right to security in the event of unemployment, sickness, disability, widowhood, old age or other lack of livelihood in circumstances beyond his control.

2. Motherhood and childhood are entitled to special care and assistance. All children, whether born in or out of wedlock, shall enjoy the same social protection.

Article 26

1. Everyone has the right to education. Education shall be free, at least in the elementary and fundamental stages. Elementary education shall be compulsory. Technical and professional education shall be made generally available and higher education shall be equally accessible to all on the basis of merit.

2. Education shall be directed to the full development of the human personality and to the strengthening of respect for human rights and fundamental freedoms. It shall promote understanding, tolerance and friendship among all nations, racial or religious groups, and shall further the activities of the United Nations for the maintenance of peace.

3. Parents have a prior right to choose the kind of education that shall be given to their children.

Article 27

1. Everyone has the right freely to participate in the cultural life of the community, to enjoy the arts and to share in scientific advancement and its benefits.

2. Everyone has the right to the protection of the moral and material interests resulting from any scientific, literary or artistic production of which he is the author.

Article 28

Everyone is entitled to a social and international order in which the rights and freedoms set forth in this Declaration can be fully realized.

Article 29

1. Everyone has duties to the community in which alone the free and full development of his personality is possible.

2. In the exercise of his rights and freedoms, everyone shall be subject only to such limitations as are determined by law solely for the purpose of securing due recognition and respect for the rights and freedoms of others and of meeting the just requirements of morality, public order and the general welfare in a democratic society.

3. These rights and freedoms may in no case be exercised contrary to the purposes and principles of the United Nations.

Article 30

Nothing in this Declaration may be interpreted as implying for any State, group or person any right to engage in any activity or to perform any act aimed at the destruction of any of the rights and freedoms set forth herein.

VII
International Covenant on Economic, Social and Cultural Rights

(1966) 993 U.N.T.S. 3, Can. T.S. 1976 No. 46, in force, including Canada, 1976

THE STATES PARTIES TO THE PRESENT COVENANT.

Considering that, in accordance with the principles proclaimed in the Charter of the United Nations, recognition of the inherent dignity and of the equal and inalienable rights of all members of the human family is the foundation of freedom, justice and peace in the world,

Recognizing that these rights derive from the inherent dignity of the human person,

Recognizing that, in accordance with the Universal Declaration of Human Rights, the ideal of free human beings enjoying freedom from fear and want can only be achieved if conditions are created whereby everyone may enjoy his economic, social and cultural rights, as well as his civil and political rights,

Considering the obligation of States under the Charter of the United Nations to promote universal respect for, and observance of, human rights and freedoms,

Realizing that the individual, having duties to other individuals to the community to which he belongs, is under a responsibility to strive for the promotion and observance of the rights recognized in the present Covenant,

Agree upon the following articles:

PART I

Article 1

1. All peoples have the right of self-determination. By virtue of that right they freely determine their political status and freely pursue their economic, social and cultural development.

2. All peoples may, for their own ends, freely dispose of their natural wealth and resources without prejudice to any obligations arising out of international economic co-operation, based upon the principle of mutual benefit, and international law. In no case may a people be deprived of its own means of subsistence.

3. The States Parties to the present Covenant, including those having responsibility for the administration of Non-Self-Governing and Trust Territories, shall promote the realization of the right of self-determination, and shall respect that right, in conformity with the provisions of the Charter of the United Nations.

PART II

Article 2

1. Each State Party to the present Covenant undertakes to take steps, individually and through international assistance and co-operation, especially economic and technical, to the maximum of its available resources, with a view to achieving progressively the full realization of the rights recognized in the present Covenant by all appropriate means, including particularly the adoption of legislative measures.

2. The States Parties to the present Covenant undertake to guarantee that the rights enunciated in the present Covenant will be exercised without discrimination of any kind as to race, colour, sex, language, religion, political or other opinion, national or social origin, property, birth or other status.

3. Developing countries, with due regard to human rights and their national economy, may determine to what extent they would guarantee the economic rights recognized in the present Covenant to non-nationals.

Article 3

The States Parties to the present Covenant undertake to ensure the equal right of men and women to the enjoyment of all economic, social and cultural rights set forth in the present Covenant.

Article 4

The States Parties to the present Covenant recognize that, in the enjoyment of those rights provided by the State in conformity with the present Covenant, the State may subject such rights only to such limitations as are determined by law only in so far as this may be compatible with the nature of these rights and solely for the purpose of promoting the general welfare in a democratic society.

Article 5

1. Nothing in the present Covenant may be interpreted as implying for any State, group or person any right to engage in any activity or to perform any act aimed at the destruction of any of the rights or freedoms recognized herein, or at their limitation to a greater extent than is provided for in the present Covenant.

2. No restriction upon or derogation from any of the fundamental human rights recognized or existing in any country in virtue of law, conventions, regulations or custom shall be admitted on the pretext that the present Covenant does not recognize such rights or that it recognizes them to a lesser extent.

PART III

Article 6

1. The States Parties to the present Covenant recognize the right to work, which includes the right of everyone to the opportunity to gain his living by work which he freely chooses or accepts, and will take appropriate steps to safeguard this right.

2. The steps to be taken by a State Party to the present Covenant to achieve the full realization of this right shall include technical and vocational guidance and training programmes, policies and techniques to achieve steady economic, social and cultural development and full and productive employment under conditions safeguarding fundamental political and economic freedoms to the individual.

Article 7

The States Parties to the present Covenant recognize the right of everyone to the enjoyment of just and favourable conditions of work which ensure, in particular:

(a) Remuneration which provides all workers, as a minimum, with:

(i) Fair wages and equal remuneration for work of equal value without distinction of any kind, in particular women being guaranteed conditions of work not inferior to those enjoyed by men, with equal pay for equal work;

(ii) A decent living for themselves and their families in accordance with the provisions of the present Covenant;

(b) Safe and healthy working conditions;

(c) Equal opportunity for everyone to be promoted in his employment to an appropriate higher level, subject to no considerations other than those of seniority and competence;

(d) Rest, leisure and reasonable limitation of working hours and periodic holidays with pay, as well as remuneration for public holidays.

Article 8

1. The States Parties to the present Covenant undertake to ensure:

(a) The right of everyone to form trade unions and join the trade union of his choice, subject only to the rules of the organization concerned, for the promotion and protection of his economic and social interests. No restrictions may be placed on the exercise of this right other than those prescribed by law and which are necessary in a democratic society in the interests of national security or public order or for the protection of the rights and freedoms of others;

(b) The right of trade unions to establish national federations or confederations and the right of the latter to form or join international trade-union organizations;

(c) The right of trade unions to function freely subject to no limitations other than those prescribed by law and which are necessary in a democratic society in the interests of national security or public order or for the protection of the rights and freedoms of others;

(d) The right to strike, provided that it is exercised in conformity with the laws of the particular country.

2. This article shall not prevent the imposition of lawful restrictions on the exercise of these rights by members of the armed forces or of the police or of the administration of the State.

3. Nothing in this article shall authorize States Parties to the International Labour Organisation Convention of 1948 concerning Freedom of Association and Protection of the Right to Organize to take legislative measures which would prejudice, or apply the law in such a manner as would prejudice, the guarantees provided for in that Convention.

Article 9

The States Parties to the present Covenant recognize the right of every one to social security, including social insurance.

Article 10

The States Parties to the present Covenant recognize that:

1. The widest possible protection and assistance should be accorded to the family, which is the natural and fundamental group unit of society, particularly for its establishment and while it is responsible for the care and education of dependent children. Marriage must be entered into with the free consent of the intending spouses.

2. Special protection should be accorded to mothers during a reasonable period before and after childbirth. During such period working mothers should be accorded paid leave or leave with adequate social security benefits.

3. Special measures of protection and assistance should be taken on behalf of all children and young persons without any discrimination for reasons of parentage or other conditions. Children and young persons should be protected from economic and social exploitation. Their employment in work harmful to their morals or health or dangerous to life or likely to hamper their normal development should be punishable by law. States should also set age limits below which the paid employment of child labour should be prohibited and punishable by law.

Article 11

1. The States Parties to the present Covenant recognize the right of everyone to an adequate standard of living for himself and his family, including adequate food, clothing and housing, and to the continuous improvement of living conditions. The States Parties will take appropriate steps to ensure the realization of this right, recognizing to this effect the essential importance of international co-operation based on free consent.

2. The States Parties to the present Covenant, recognizing the fundamental right of everyone to be free from hunger, shall take, individually and through international co-operation, the measures, including specific programmes, which are needed:

(a) To improve methods of production, conservation and distribution of food by making full use of technical and scientific knowledge, by disseminating knowledge of the principles of nutrition and by developing or reforming agrarian systems in such a way as to achieve the most efficient development and utilization of natural resources;

(b) Taking into account the problems of both food-importing and food-exporting countries, to ensure an equitable distribution of world food supplies in relation to need.

Article 12

1. The States Parties to the present Covenant recognize the right of everyone to the enjoyment of the highest attainable standard of physical and mental health.

2. The steps to be taken by the States Parties to the present Covenant to achieve the full realization of this right shall include those necessary for:

(a) The provision for the reduction of the stillbirth-rate and of infant mortality and for the healthy development of the child;

(b) The improvement of all aspects of environmental and industrial hygiene;

(c) The prevention, treatment and control of epidemic, endemic, occupational and other diseases;

(d) The creation of conditions which would assure to all medical service and medical attention in the event of sickness.

Article 13

1. The States Parties to the present Covenant recognize the right of everyone to education. They agree that education shall be directed to the full development of the human personality and the sense of its dignity, and shall strengthen the respect for human rights and fundamental freedoms. They further agree that education shall enable all persons to participate effectively

in a free society, promote understanding, tolerance and friendship among all nations and all racial, ethnic or religious groups, and further the activities of the United Nations for the maintenance of peace.

2. The States Parties to the present Covenant recognize that, with a view to achieving the full realization of this right:

(a) Primary education shall be compulsory and available free to all;

(b) Secondary education in its different forms, including technical and vocational secondary education, shall be made generally available and accessible to all by every appropriate means, and in particular by the progressive introduction of free education;

(c) Higher education shall be made equally accessible to all, on the basis of capacity, by every appropriate means, and in particular by the progressive introduction of free education;

(d) Fundamental education shall be encouraged or intensified as far as possible for those persons who have not received or completed the whole period of their primary education;

(e) The development of a system of schools at all levels shall be actively pursued, an adequate fellowship system shall be established, and the material conditions of teaching staff shall be continuously improved.

3. The States Parties to the present Covenant undertake to have respect for the liberty of parents and, when applicable, legal guardians to choose for their children schools, other than those established by the public authorities, which conform to such minimum educational standards as may be laid down or approved by the State and to ensure the religious and moral education of their children in conformity with their own convictions.

4. No part of this article shall be construed so as to interfere with the liberty of individuals and bodies to establish and direct educational institutions, subject always to the observance of the principles set forth in paragraph 1 of this article and to the requirement that the education given in such institutions shall conform to such minimum standards as may be laid down by the State.

Article 14

Each State Party to the present Covenant which, at the time of becoming a Party, has not been able to secure in its metropolitan territory or other territories under its jurisdiction compulsory primary education, free of charge, undertakes, within two years, to work out and adopt a detailed plan of action for the progressive implementation, within a reasonable number of years, to be fixed in the plan, of the principle of compulsory education free of charge for all.

Article 15

1. The States Parties to the present Covenant recognize the right of everyone:

(a) To take part in cultural life;

(b) To enjoy the benefits of scientific progress and its applications;

(c) To benefit from the protection of the moral and material interests resulting from any scientific, literary or artistic production of which he is the author.

2. The steps to be taken by the States Parties to the present Covenant to achieve the full realization of this right shall include those necessary for the conservation, the development and the diffusion of science and culture.

3. The States Parties to the present Covenant undertake to respect the freedom indispensable for scientific research and creative activity.

4. The States Parties to the present Covenant recognize the benefits to be derived from the encouragement and development of international contacts and co-operation in the scientific and cultural fields.

PART IV

Article 16

1. The States Parties to the present Covenant undertake to submit in conformity with this part of the Covenant reports on the measures which they have adopted and the progress made in achieving the observance of the rights recognized herein.

2. (a) All reports shall be submitted to the Secretary-General of the United Nations, who shall transmit copies to the Economic and Social Council for consideration in accordance with the provisions of the present Covenant.

(b) The Secretary-General of the United Nations shall also transmit to the specialized agencies copies of the reports, or any relevant parts therefrom, from States Parties to the present Covenant which are also members of these specialized agencies in so far as these reports, or parts therefrom, relate to any matters which fall within the responsibilities of the said agencies in accordance with their constitutional instruments.

Article 17

1. The States Parties to the present Covenant shall furnish their reports in stages, in accordance with a programme to be established by the Economic and Social Council within one year of the entry into force of the present Covenant after consultation with the States Parties and the specialized agencies concerned.

2. Reports may indicate factors and difficulties affecting the degree of fulfilment of obligations under the present Covenant.

3. Where relevant information has previously been furnished to the United Nations or to any specialized agency by any State Party to the present Covenant, it will not be necessary to reproduce that information, but a precise reference to the information so furnished will suffice.

Article 18

Pursuant to its responsibilities under the Charter of the United Nations in the field of human rights and fundamental freedoms, the Economic and Social Council may make arrangements with the specialized agencies in respect of their reporting to it on the progress made in achieving the observance of the provisions of the present Covenant falling within the scope of their activities. These reports may include particulars of decisions and recommendations on such implementation adopted by their competent organs.

Article 19

The Economic and Social Council may transmit to the Commission on Human Rights for study and general recommendation or as appropriate for information the reports concerning human rights submitted by States in accordance with Articles 16 and 17, and those concerning human rights submitted by the specialized agencies in accordance with Article 18.

• • •

Article 21

The Economic and Social Council may submit from time to time to the General Assembly reports with recommendations of a general nature and a summary of the information received from the States Parties to the present Covenant and the specialized agencies on the measures taken and the progress made in achieving general observance of the rights recognized in the present Covenant.

• • •

Article 23

The States Parties to the present Covenant agree that international action for the achievement of the rights recognized in the present Covenant includes such methods as the conclusion of conventions, the adoption of recommendations, the furnishing of technical assistance and the holding of regional meetings and technical meetings for the purpose of consultation and study organized in conjunction with the Governments concerned.

• • •

PART V

Article 25

Nothing in the present Covenant shall be interpreted as impairing the inherent right of all peoples to enjoy and utilize fully and freely their natural wealth and resources.

• • •

Article 28

The provisions of the present Covenant shall extend to all parts of federal States without any limitations or exceptions.

VIII
International Covenant on Civil and Political Rights

(1966) 999 U.N.T.S. 171, Can. T.S. 1976 No. 47, in force, including Canada, 1976

THE STATES PARTIES TO THE PRESENT COVENANT,

Considering that, in accordance with the principles proclaimed in the Charter of the United Nations, recognition of the inherent dignity and of the equal and inalienable rights of all members of the human family is the foundation of freedom, justice and peace in the world,

Recognizing that these rights derive from the inherent dignity of the human person,

Recognizing that, in accordance with the Universal Declaration of Human Rights, the ideal of free human beings enjoying civil and political freedom and freedom from fear and want can only be achieved if conditions are created whereby everyone may enjoy his civil and political rights, as well as his economic, social and cultural rights,

Considering the obligation of States under the Charter of the United Nations to promote universal respect for, and observance of, human rights and freedoms,

Realizing that the individual, having duties to other individuals and to the community to which he belongs, is under a responsibility to strive for the promotion and observance of the rights recognized in the present Covenant,

Agree upon the following articles:

PART I

Article 1

1. All peoples have the right of self-determination. By virtue of that right they freely determine their political status and freely pursue their economic, social and cultural development.

2. All peoples may, for their own ends, freely dispose of their natural wealth and resources without prejudice to any obligations arising out of international economic co-operation, based upon the principle of mutual benefit, and international law. In no case may a people be deprived of its own means of subsistence.

3. The States Parties to the present Covenant, including those having responsibility for the administration of Non-Self-Governing and Trust Territories, shall promote the realization of the right of self-determination, and shall respect that right, in conformity with the provisions of the Charter of the United Nations.

PART II

Article 2

1. Each State Party to the present Covenant undertakes to respect and to ensure to all individuals within its territory and subject to its jurisdiction the rights recognized in the present Covenant, without distinction of any kind, such as race, colour, sex, language, religion, political or other opinion, national or social origin, property, birth or other status.

2. Where not already provided for by existing legislative or other measures, each State Party to the present Covenant undertakes to take the necessary steps, in accordance with its

constitutional processes and with the provisions of the present Covenant, to adopt such legislative or other measures as may be necessary to give effect to the rights recognized in the present Covenant.

3. Each State Party to the present Covenant undertakes:

(a) To ensure that any person whose rights or freedoms as herein recognized are violated shall have an effective remedy, notwithstanding that the violation has been committed by persons acting in an official capacity;

(b) To ensure that any person claiming such a remedy shall have his right thereto determined by competent judicial, administrative or legislative authorities, or by any other competent authority provided for by the legal system of the State, and to develop the possibilities of judicial remedy;

(c) To ensure that the competent authorities shall enforce such remedies when granted.

Article 3

The States Parties to the present Covenant undertake to ensure the equal right of men and women to the enjoyment of all civil and political rights set forth in the present Covenant.

Article 4

1. In time of public emergency which threatens the life of the nation and the existence of which is officially proclaimed, the States Parties to the present Covenant may take measures derogating from their obligations under the present Covenant to the extent strictly required by the exigencies of the situation, provided that such measures are not inconsistent with their other obligations under international law and do not involve discrimination solely on the ground of race, colour, sex, language, religion or social origin.

2. No derogation from articles 6, 7, 8 (paragraphs 1 and 2), 11, 15, 16 and 18 may be made under this provision.

3. Any State Party to the present Covenant availing itself of the right of derogation shall immediately inform the other States Parties to the present Covenant, through the intermediary of the Secretary-General of the United Nations, of the provisions from which it has derogated and of the reasons by which it was actuated. A further communication shall be made, through the same intermediary, on the date on which it terminates such derogation.

Article 5

1. Nothing in the present Covenant may be interpreted as implying for any State, group or person any right to engage in any activity or perform any act aimed at the destruction of any of the rights and freedoms recognized herein or at their limitation to a greater extent than is provided for in the present Covenant.

2. There shall be no restriction upon or derogation from any of the fundamental human rights recognized or existing in any State Party to the present Covenant pursuant to law, conventions, regulations or custom on the pretext that the present Covenant does not recognize such rights or that it recognizes them to a lesser extent.

PART III

Article 6

1. Every human being has the inherent right to life. This right shall be protected by law. No one shall be arbitrarily deprived of his life.

2. In countries which have not abolished the death penalty, sentence of death may be imposed only for the most serious crimes in accordance with the law in force at the time of the commission of the crime and not contrary to the provisions of the present Covenant and to the Convention on the Prevention and Punishment of the Crime of Genocide. This penalty can only be carried out pursuant to a final judgment rendered by a competent court.

3. When deprivation of life constitutes the crime of genocide, it is understood that nothing in this article shall authorize any State Party to the present Covenant to derogate in any way from any obligation assumed under the provisions of the Convention on the Prevention and Punishment of the Crime of Genocide.

4. Anyone sentenced to death shall have the right to seek pardon or commutation of the sentence. Amnesty, pardon or commutation of the sentence of death may be granted in all cases.

5. Sentence of death shall not be imposed for crimes committed by persons below eighteen years of age and shall not be carried out on pregnant women.

6. Nothing in this article shall be invoked to delay or to prevent the abolition of capital punishment by any State Party to the present Covenant.

Article 7

No one shall be subjected to torture or to cruel, inhuman or degrading treatment or punishment. In particular, no one shall be subjected without his free consent to medical or scientific experimentation.

Article 8

1. No one shall be held in slavery; slavery and the slave-trade in all their forms shall be prohibited.

2. No one shall be held in servitude.

3. (a) No one shall be required to perform forced or compulsory labour;

(b) Paragraph 3(a) shall not be held to preclude, in countries where imprisonment with hard labour may be imposed as a punishment for a crime, the performance of hard labour in pursuance of a sentence to such punishment by a competent court;

(c) For the purpose of this paragraph the term "forced or compulsory labour" shall not include:

(i) Any work or service, not referred to in subparagraph (b), normally required of a person who is under detention in consequence of a lawful order of a court, or of a person during conditional release from such detention;

(ii) Any service of a military character and, in countries where conscientious objection is recognized, any national service required by law of conscientious objectors;

(iii) Any service exacted in cases of emergency or calamity threatening the life or well-being of the community;

(iv) Any work or service which forms part of normal civil obligations.

Article 9

1. Everyone has the right to liberty and security of person. No one shall be subjected to arbitrary arrest or detention. No one shall be deprived of his liberty except on such grounds and in accordance with such procedure as are established by law.

2. Anyone who is arrested shall be informed, at the time of arrest, of the reasons for his arrest and shall be promptly informed of any charges against him.

3. Anyone arrested or detained on a criminal charge shall be brought promptly before a judge or other officer authorized by law to exercise judicial power and shall be entitled to trial within a reasonable time or to release. It shall not be the general rule that persons awaiting trial shall be detained in custody, but release may be subject to guarantees to appear for trial, at any other stage of the judicial proceedings, and, should occasion arise, for execution of the judgment.

4. Anyone who is deprived of his liberty by arrest or detention shall be entitled to take proceedings before a court, in order that that court may decide without delay on the lawfulness of his detention and order his release if the detention is not lawful.

5. Anyone who has been the victim of unlawful arrest or detention shall have an enforceable right to compensation.

Article 10

1. All persons deprived of their liberty shall be treated with humanity and with respect for the inherent dignity of the human person.

2. (a) Accused persons shall, save in exceptional circumstances, be segregated from convicted persons and shall be subject to separate treatment appropriate to their status as unconvicted persons;

(b) Accused juvenile persons shall be separated from adults and brought as speedily as possible for adjudication.

3. The penitentiary system shall comprise treatment of prisoners the essential aim of which shall be their reformation and social rehabilitation. Juvenile offenders shall be segregated from adults and be accorded treatment appropriate to their age and legal status.

Article 11

No one shall be imprisoned merely on the ground of inability to fulfil a contractual obligation.

Article 12

1. Everyone lawfully within the territory of a State shall, within that territory, have the right to liberty of movement and freedom to choose his residence.

2. Everyone shall be free to leave any country, including his own.

3. The above-mentioned rights shall not be subject to any restrictions except those which are provided by law, are necessary to protect national security, public order (*ordre public*), public health or morals or the rights and freedoms of others, and are consistent with the other rights recognized in the present Covenant.

4. No one shall be arbitrarily deprived of the right to enter his own country.

Article 13

An alien lawfully in the territory of a State Party to the present Covenant may be expelled therefrom only in pursuance of a decision reached in accordance with law and shall, except where compelling reasons of national security otherwise require, be allowed to submit the reasons against his expulsion and to have his case reviewed by, and be represented for the purpose before, the competent authority or a person or persons especially designated by the competent authority.

Article 14

1. All persons shall be equal before the courts and tribunals. In the determination of any criminal charge against him, or of his rights and obligations in a suit of law, everyone shall be entitled to a fair and public hearing of a competent, independent and impartial tribunal established by law. The Press and the public may be excluded from all or part of a trial for reasons of morals, public order (*ordre public*) or national security in a democratic society, or when the interest of the private lives of the parties so requires, or the extent strictly necessary in the opinion of the court in special circumstances where publicity would prejudice the interests of justice; but any judgment tendered in a criminal case or in a suit at law shall be made public except where the interest of juvenile persons otherwise requires or the proceedings concern matrimonial disputes or the guardianship of children.

2. Everyone charged with a criminal offence shall have the right to be presumed innocent until proved guilty according to law.

3. In the determination of any criminal charge against him, everyone shall be entitled to the following minimum guarantees, in full equality:

(a) To be informed promptly and in detail in a language which he understands of the nature and cause of the charge against him;

(b) To have adequate time and facilities for the preparation of his defence and to communicate with counsel of his own choosing;

(c) To be tried without undue delay;

(d) To be tried in his presence, and to defend himself in person or through legal assistance of his own choosing; to be informed, if he does not have legal assistance, of this right; and to have legal assistance assigned to him, in any case where the interests of justice so require, and without payment by him in any such case if he does not have sufficient means to pay for it;

(e) to examine, or have examined, the witnesses against him and to obtain the attendance and examination of witnesses on his behalf under the same conditions as witnesses against him;

(f) To have the free assistance of an interpreter if he cannot understand or speak the language used in court;

(g) Not to be compelled to testify against himself or to confess guilt.

4. In the case of juvenile persons, the procedure shall be suchs as will take account of their age and the desirability of promoting their rehabilitation.

5. Everyone convicted of a crime shall have the right to his conviction and sentence being reviewed by a higher tribunal according to law.

6. When a person has by a final decision been convicted of a criminal offence and when subsequently his conviction has been reversed or he has been pardoned on the ground that a new or newly discovered fact shows conclusively that there has been a miscarriage of justice, the person who has suffered punishment as a result of such conviction shall be compensated according to law, unless it is proved that the non-disclosure of the unknown fact in time is wholly or partly attributable to him.

7. No one shall be liable to be tried or punished again for an offence for which he has already been finally convicted or acquitted in accordance with the law and penal procedure of each country.

Article 15

1. No one shall be held guilty of any criminal offence on account of any act or omission which did not constitute a criminal offence, under national or international law, at the time when it was committed. Nor shall a heavier penalty be imposed than the one that was applicable at the time when the criminal offence was committed. If, subsequent to the commission of the offence, provision is made by law for imposition of a lighter penalty, the offender shall benefit thereby.

2. Nothing in this article shall prejudice the trial and punishment of any person for any act or omission which, at the time when it was committed, was criminal according to the general principles of law recognized by the community of nations.

Article 16

Everyone shall have the right to recognition everywhere as a person before the law.

Article 17

1. No one shall be subject to arbitrary or unlawful interference with his privacy, family, home or correspondence, nor to unlawful attacks on his honour and reputation.

2. Everyone has the right to the protection of the law against such interference or attacks.

Article 18

1. Everyone shall have the right to freedom of thought, conscience and religion. This right shall include freedom to have or to adopt a religion or belief of his choice, and freedom, either individually or in community with others and in public or private, to manifest his religion or belief in worship, observance, practice and teaching.

2. No one shall be subject to coercion which would impair his freedom to have or to adopt a religion or belief of his choice.

3. Freedom to manifest one's religion or beliefs may be subject only to such limitations as are prescribed by law and are necessary to protect public safety, order, health, or morals or the fundamental rights and freedoms of others.

4. The States Parties to the present Covenant undertake to have respect for the liberty of parents and, when applicable, legal guardians to ensure the religious and moral education of their children in conformity with their own convictions.

Article 19

1. Everyone shall have the right to hold opinions without interference.

2. Everyone shall have the right to freedom of expression; this right shall include freedom to seek, receive and impart information and ideas of all kinds, regardless of frontiers, either orally, in writing or in print, in the form of art, or through any other media of his choice.

3. The exercise of the rights provided for in paragraph 2 of this article carries with it special duties and responsibilities. It may therefore be subject to certain restrictions, but these shall only be such as are provided by law and are necessary:

(a) For respect of the rights or reputations of others;

(b) For the protection of national security or of public order (*ordre public*), or of public health or morals.

Article 20

1. Any propaganda for war shall be prohibited by law.

2. Any advocacy of national, racial or religious hatred that constitutes incitement to discrimination, hostility or violence shall be prohibited by law.

Article 21

The right of peaceful assembly shall be recognized. No restrictions may be placed on the exercise of this right other than those imposed in conformity with the law and which are necessary in a democratic society in the interests of national security or public safety, public order (*ordre public*), the protection of public health or morals or the protection of the rights and freedoms of others.

Article 22

1. Everyone shall have the right to freedom of association with others, including the right to form and join trade unions for the protection of his interests.

2. No restrictions may be placed on the exercise of this right other than those which are prescribed by law and which are necessary in a democratic society in the interests of national security or public safety, public order (*ordre public*), the protection of public health or morals or the protection of the rights and freedoms of others. This article shall not prevent the imposition of lawful restrictions on members of the armed forces and of the police in their exercise of this right.

3. Nothing in this article shall authorize States Parties to the International Labour Organisation Convention of 1948 concerning Freedom of Association and Protection of the Right to Organize to take legislative measures which would prejudice, or to apply the law in such a manner as to prejudice, the guarantees provided for in that Convention.

Article 23

1. The family is the natural and fundamental group unit of society and is entitled to protection by society and the State.

2. The right of men and women of marriageable age to marry and to found a family shall be recognized.

3. No marriage shall be entered into without the free and full consent of the intending spouses.

4. State Parties to the present Covenants shall take appropriate steps to ensure equality of rights and responsibilities of spouses as to marriage, during marriage and at its disolution. On the case of dissolution, provision shall be made for the necessary protection of any children.

Article 24

1. Every child shall have, without any discrimination as to race, colour, sex, language, religion, national or social origin, property or birth, the right to such measures of protection as are required by his status as a minor, on the part of his family, society and the State.

2. Every child shall be registered immediately after birth and shall have a name.

3. Every child has the right to acquire a nationality.

Article 25
Every citizen shall have the right and the opportunity, without any of the distinctions mentioned in article 2 and without unreasonable restrictions:

(a) To take part in the conduct of public affairs, directly or through freely chosen representatives;

(b) To vote and to be elected at genuine periodic elections which shall be by universal and equal suffrage and shall be held by secret ballot, guaranteeing the free expression of the will of the electors;

(c) To have access, on general terms of equality, to public service in his country.

Article 26
All persons are equal before the law and are entitled without any discrimination to the equal protection of the law. In this respect, the law shall prohibit any discrimination and guarantee to all persons equal and effective protection against discrimination on any ground such as race, colour, sex, language, religion, political or other opinion, national or social origin, property, birth or other status.

Article 27
In those States in which ethnic, religious or linguistic minorities exist, persons belonging to such minorities shall not be denied the right, in community with the other members of their group, to enjoy their own culture, to profess and practice their own religion, or to use their own language.

PART IV

Article 28
1. There shall be established a Human Rights Committee (hereafter referred to in the present Covenant as the Committee). It shall consist of eighteen members and shall carry out the functions hereinafter provided.

2. The Committee shall be composed of nationals of the States Parties to the present Covenant who shall be persons of high moral character and recognized competence in the field of human rights, consideration being given to the usefulness of the participation of some persons having legal experience.

3. The members of the Committee shall be elected and shall serve in their personal capacity.

• • •

Article 40
1. The States Parties to the present Covenant undertake to submit reports on the measures they have adopted which give effect to the rights recognized herein and on the progress made in the enjoyment of those rights:

(a) Within one year of the entry into force of the present Covenant for the States Parties concerned;

(b) Thereafter whenever the Committee so requests.

2. All reports shall be submitted to the Secretary-General of the United Nations, who shall transmit them to the Committee for consideration. Reports shall indicate the factors and difficulties, if any, affecting the implementation of the present Covenant.

3. The Secretary-General of the United Nations may, after consultation with the Committee, transmit to the specialized agencies concerned copies of such parts of the reports as may fall within their field of competence.

4. The Committee shall study the reports submitted by the States Parties to the present Covenant. It shall transmit its reports, and such general comments as it may consider appropriate, to the States Parties. The Committee may also transmit to the Economic and Social Council these comments along with the copies of the reports it has received from States Parties to the present Covenant.

5. The States Parties to the present Covenant may submit to the Committee observations on any comments that may be made in accordance with paragraph 4 of this article.

Article 41

1. A State Party to the present Covenant may at any time declare under this article that it recognizes the competence of the Committee to receive and consider communications to the effect that a State Party claims that another State Party is not fulfilling its obligations under the present Covenant. Communications under this article may be received and considered only if submitted by a State Party which has made a declaration recognizing in regard to itself the competence of the Committee. No communication shall be received by the Committee if it concerns a State Party which has not made such a declaration. Communications received under this article shall be dealt with in accordance with the following procedure:

(a) If a State Party to the present Covenant considers that another State Party is not giving effect to the provisions of the present Covenant, it may, by written communication, bring the matter to the attention of that State Party. Within three months after the receipt of the communication, the receiving State shall afford the State which sent the communication an explanation or any other statement in writing clarifying the matter, which should include, to the extent possible and pertinent, reference to domestic procedures and remedies taken, pending, or available in the matter.

(b) If the matter is not adjusted to the satisfaction of both States Parties concerned within six months after the receipt by the receiving State of the initial communication, either State shall have the right to refer the matter to the Committee, by notice given to the Committee and to the other State.

(c) The Committee shall deal with a matter referred to it only after it has ascertained that all available domestic remedies have been invoked and exhausted in the matter, in conformity with the generally recognized principles of international law. This shall not be the rule where the application of the remedies is unreasonably prolonged.

(d) The Committee shall hold closed meetings when examining communications under this article.

(e) Subject to the provisions of sub-paragraph (c), the Committee shall make available its good offices to the States Parties concerned with a view to a friendly solution of the matter on the basis of respect for human rights and fundamental freedoms as recognized in the present Covenant.

(f) In any matter referred to it, the Committee may call upon the States Parties concerned, referred to in sub-paragraph (b), to supply any relevant information.

(g) The States Parties concerned, referred to in sub-paragraph (b), shall have the right to be represented when the matter is being considered in the Committee and to make submissions orally and/or in writing.

(h) The Committee shall, within twelve months after the date of receipt of notice under sub-paragraph (b), submit a report:

(i) If a solution within the terms of sub-paragraph (e) is reached, the Committee shall confine its report to a brief statement of the facts and of the solution reached;

(ii) If a solution within the terms of sub-paragraph (e) is not reached, the Committee shall confine its report to a brief statement of the facts; the written submissions and record of the oral submissions made by the States Parties concerned shall be attached to the report.

In every matter, the report shall be communicated to the States Parties concerned.

2. The provisions of this article shall come into force when ten States Parties to the present Covenant have made declarations under paragraph 1 of this article. Such declarations shall be deposited by the States Parties with the Secretary-General of the United Nations, who shall transmit copies thereof to the other States Parties. A declaration may be withdrawn at any time by notification to the Secretary-General. Such a withdrawal shall not prejudice the consideration of any matter which is the subject of a communication already transmitted under this article; no further communication by any State Party shall be received after the notification of withdrawal of the declaration has been received by the Secretary-General, unless the State Party concerned had made a new declaration.

• • •

Article 45
The Committee shall submit to the General Assembly of the United Nations through the Economic and Social Council, an annual report on its activities.

• • •

PART V

Article 47
Nothing in the present Covenant shall be interpreted as impairing the inherent right of all peoples to enjoy and utilize fully and freely their natural wealth and resources.

• • •

PART VI

Article 50
The provisions of the present Covenant shall extend to all parts of federal States without any limitations or exceptions.

IX

United Nations Convention on
the Law of the Sea

UN Doc. A/CONF. 62/122 (1982), in force 1994, and for Canada 2003

PART I
INTRODUCTION

Article 1

Use of terms and scope

1. For the purposes of this Convention:

(1) "Area" means the sea-bed and ocean floor and subsoil thereof, beyond the limits of national jurisdiction;

(2) "Authority" means the International Sea-Bed Authority;

(3) "activities in the Area" means all activities of exploration for, and exploitation of, the resources of the Area;

(4) "pollution of the marine environment" means the introduction by man, directly or indirectly, of substances or energy into the marine environment, including estuaries, which results or is likely to result in such deleterious effects as harm to living resources and marine life, hazards to human health, hindrance to marine activities, including fishing and other legitimate uses of the sea, impairment of quality for use of sea water and reduction of amenities;

(5) (a) "dumping" means:

(i) any deliberate disposal of wastes or other matter from vessels, aircraft, platforms or other man-made structures at sea;

(ii) any deliberate disposal of vessels, aircraft, platforms or other man-made structures at sea;

(b) "dumping" does not include:

(i) the disposal of wastes or other matter incidental to, or derived from the normal operations of vessels, aircraft, platforms or other man-made structures at sea and their equipment, other than wastes or other matter transported by or to vessels, aircraft, platforms or other man-made structures at sea, operating for the purpose of disposal of such matter or derived from the treatment of such wastes or other matter on such vessels, aircraft, platforms or structures;

(ii) placement of matter for a purpose other than the mere disposal thereof, provided that such placement is not contrary to the aims of this Convention.

2. (1) "States Parties" means States which have consented to be bound by this Convention and for which this Convention is in force. ...

PART II
TERRITORIAL SEA AND CONTIGUOUS ZONE

SECTION 1. GENERAL PROVISIONS

Article 2

*Legal status of the territorial sea, of the air space over
the territorial sea and of its bed and subsoil*

1. The sovereignty of a coastal State extends, beyond its land territory and internal waters and, in the case of an archipelagic State, its archipelagic waters, to an adjacent belt of sea, described as the territorial sea.

2. This sovereignty extends to the air space over the territorial sea as well as to its bed and subsoil.

3. The sovereignty over the territorial sea is exercised subject to this Convention and to other rules of international law.

SECTION 2. LIMITS OF THE TERRITORIAL SEA

Article 3

Breadth of the territorial sea

Every State has the right to establish the breadth of its territorial sea up to a limit not exceeding 12 nautical miles, measured from baselines determined in accordance with this Convention.

Article 4

Outer limit of the territorial sea

The outer limit of the territorial sea is the line every point of which is at a distance from the nearest point of the baseline equal to the breadth of the territorial sea.

Article 5

Normal baseline

Except where otherwise provided in this Convention, the normal baseline for measuring the breadth of the territorial sea is the low-water line along the coast as marked on large-scale charts officially recognized by the coastal State.

Article 6

Reefs

In the case of islands situated on atolls or of islands having fringing reefs, the baseline for measuring the breadth of the territorial sea is the seaward low-water line of the reef, as shown by the appropriate symbol on charts officially recognized by the coastal State.

Article 7

Straight baselines

1. In localities where the coastline is deeply indented and cut into, or if there is a fringe of islands along the coast in its immediate vicinity, the method of straight baselines joining

appropriate points may be employed in drawing the baseline from which the breadth of the territorial sea is measured.

2. Where because of the presence of a delta and other natural conditions the coastline is highly unstable, the appropriate points may be selected along the furthest seaward extent of the low-water line and, notwithstanding subsequent regression of the low-water line, the straight baselines shall remain effective until changed by the coastal State in accordance with this Convention.

3. The drawing of straight baselines must not depart to any appreciable extent from the general direction of the coast, and the sea areas lying within the lines must be sufficiently closely linked to the land domain to be subject to the régime of internal waters.

4. Straight baselines shall not be drawn to and from low-tide elevations, unless lighthouses or similar installations which are permanently above sea level have been built on them or except in instances where the drawing of baselines to and from such elevations has received general international recognition.

5. Where the method of straight baselines is applicable under paragraph 1, account may be taken, in determining particular baselines, of economic interests peculiar to the region concerned, the reality and the importance of which are clearly evidenced by long usage.

6. The system of straight baselines may not be applied by a State in such a manner as to cut off the territorial sea of another State from the high seas or an exclusive economic zone.

Article 8

Internal waters

1. Except as provided in Part IV, waters on the landward side of the baseline of the territorial sea form part of the internal waters of the State.

2. Where the establishment of a straight baseline in accordance with the method set forth in article 7 has the effect of enclosing as internal waters areas which had not previously been considered as such, a right of innocent passage as provided in this Convention shall exist in those waters.

Article 9

Mouths of rivers

If a river flows directly into the sea, the baseline shall be a straight line across the mouth of the river between points on the low-water line of its banks.

Article 10

Bays

1. This article relates only to bays the coasts of which belong to a single State.

2. For the purposes of this Convention, a bay is a well-marked indentation whose penetration is in such proportion to the width of its mouth as to contain land-locked waters and constitute more than a mere curvature of the coast. An indentation shall not, however, be regarded as a bay unless its area is as large as, or larger than, that of the semi-circle whose diameter is a line drawn across the mouth of that indentation.

3. For the purpose of measurement, the area of an indentation is that lying between the low-water mark around the shore of the indentation and a line joining the low-water mark of its

natural entrance points. Where, because of the presence of islands, an indentation has more than one mouth, the semi-circle shall be drawn on a line as long as the sum total of the lengths of the lines across the different mouths. Islands within an indentation shall be included as if they were part of the water area of the indentation.

4. If the distance between the low-water marks of the natural entrance points of a bay does not exceed 24 nautical miles, a closing line may be drawn between these two low-water marks, and the waters enclosed thereby shall be considered as internal waters.

5. Where the distance between the low-water marks of the natural entrance points of a bay exceeds 24 nautical miles, a straight baseline of 24 nautical miles shall be drawn within the bay in such a manner as to enclose the maximum area of water that is possible with a line of that length.

6. The foregoing provisions do not apply to so-called "historic" bays, or in any case where the system of straight baselines provided for in article 7 is applied.

Article 11

Ports

For the purpose of delimiting the territorial sea, the outermost permanent harbour works which form an integral part of the harbour system are regarded as forming part of the coast. Off-shore installations and artificial islands shall not be considered as permanent harbour works.

Article 12

Roadsteads

Roadsteads which are normally used for the loading, unloading and anchoring of ships, and which would otherwise be situated wholly or partly outside the outer limit of the territorial sea, are included in the territorial sea.

Article 13

Low-tide elevations

1. A low-tide elevation is a naturally formed area of land which is surrounded by and above water at low tide but submerged at high tide. Where a low-tide elevation is situated wholly or partly at a distance not exceeding the breadth of the territorial sea from the mainland or an island, the low-water line on that elevation may be used as the baseline for measuring the breadth of the territorial sea.

2. Where a low-tide elevation is wholly situated at a distance exceeding the breadth of the territorial sea from the mainland or an island, it has no territorial sea of its own.

Article 14

Combination of methods for determining baselines

The coastal State may determine baselines in turn by any of the methods provided for in the foregoing articles to suit different conditions.

Article 15

Delimitation of the territorial sea between States with opposite or adjacent coasts
Where the coasts of two States are opposite or adjacent to each other, neither of the two States is entitled, failing agreement between them to the contrary, to extend its territorial sea beyond the median line every point of which is equidistant from the nearest points on the baselines from which the breadth of the territorial seas of each of the two States is measured. The above provision does not apply, however, where it is necessary by reason of historic title or other special circumstances to delimit the territorial seas of the two States in a way which is at variance therewith. …

SECTION 3. INNOCENT PASSAGE IN THE TERRITORIAL SEA

SUBSECTION A. RULES APPLICABLE TO ALL SHIPS

Article 17

Right of innocent passage
Subject to this Convention, ships of all States, whether coastal or land-locked, enjoy the right of innocent passage through the territorial sea.

Article 18

Meaning of passage
1. Passage means navigation through the territorial sea for the purpose of:
    (a) traversing that sea without entering internal waters or calling at a roadstead or port facility outside internal waters; or
    (b) proceeding to or from internal waters or a call at such roadstead or port facility.
2. Passage shall be continuous and expeditious. However, passage includes stopping and anchoring, but only in so far as the same are incidental to ordinary navigation or are rendered necessary by *force majeure* or distress or for the purpose of rendering assistance to persons, ships or aircraft in danger or distress.

Article 19

Meaning of innocent passage
1. Passage is innocent so long as it is not prejudicial to the peace, good order or security of the coastal State. Such passage shall take place in conformity with this Convention and with other rules of international law.
2. Passage of a foreign ship shall be considered to be prejudicial to the peace, good order or security of the coastal State if in the territorial sea it engages in any of the following activities:
    (a) any threat or use of force against the sovereignty, territorial integrity or political independence of the coastal State, or in any other manner in violation of the principles of international law embodied in the Charter of the United Nations;
    (b) any exercise or practice with weapons of any kind;

(c) any act aimed at collecting information to the prejudice of the defence or security of the coastal State;

(d) any act of propaganda aimed at affecting the defence or security of the coastal State;

(e) the launching, landing or taking on board of any aircraft;

(f) the launching, landing or taking on board of any military device;

(g) the loading or unloading of any commodity, currency or person contrary to the customs, fiscal, immigration or sanitary laws and regulations of the coastal State;

(h) any act of wilful and serious pollution contrary to this Convention;

(i) any fishing activities;

(j) the carrying out of research or survey activities;

(k) any act aimed at interfering with any systems of communication or any other facilities or installations of the coastal State;

(l) any other activity not having a direct bearing on passage.

Article 20

Submarines and other underwater vehicles

In the territorial sea, submarines and other underwater vehicles are required to navigate on the surface and to show their flag.

Article 21

Laws and regulations of the coastal State relating to innocent passage

1. The coastal State may adopt laws and regulations, in conformity with the provisions of this Convention and other rules of international law, relating to innocent passage through the territorial sea, in respect of all or any of the following:

(a) the safety of navigation and the regulation of maritime traffic;

(b) the protection of navigational aids and facilities and other facilities or installations;

(c) the protection of cables and pipelines;

(d) the conservation of the living resources of the sea;

(e) the prevention of infringement of the fisheries laws and regulations of the coastal State;

(f) the preservation of the environment of the coastal State and the prevention, reduction and control of pollution thereof;

(g) marine scientific research and hydrographic surveys;

(h) the prevention of infringement of the customs, fiscal, immigration or sanitary laws and regulations of the coastal State.

2. Such laws and regulations shall not apply to the design, construction, manning or equipment of foreign ships unless they are giving effect to generally accepted international rules or standards.

3. The coastal State shall give due publicity to all such laws and regulations.

4. Foreign ships exercising the right of innocent passage through the territorial sea shall comply with all such laws and regulations and all generally accepted international regulations relating to the prevention of collisions at sea.

Article 22

Sea lanes and traffic separation schemes in the territorial sea

1. The coastal State may, where necessary having regard to the safety of navigation, require foreign ships exercising the right of innocent passage through its territorial sea to use such sea lanes and traffic separation schemes as it may designate or prescribe for the regulation of the passage of ships.

2. In particular, tankers, nuclear-powered ships and ships carrying nuclear or other inherently dangerous or noxious substances or materials may be required to confine their passage to such sea lanes.

3. In the designation of sea lanes and the prescription of traffic separation schemes under this article, the coastal State shall take into account:

(a) the recommendations of the competent international organization;

(b) any channels customarily used for international navigation;

(c) the special characteristics of particular ships and channels; and

(d) the density of traffic.

4. The coastal State shall clearly indicate such sea lanes and traffic separation schemes on charts to which due publicity shall be given.

Article 23

Foreign nuclear-powered ships and ships carrying nuclear or other inherently dangerous or noxious substances

Foreign nuclear-powered ships and ships carrying nuclear or other inherently dangerous or noxious substances shall, when exercising the right of innocent passage through the territorial sea, carry documents and observe special precautionary measures established for such ships by international agreements.

Article 24

Duties of the coastal State

1. The coastal State shall not hamper the innocent passage of foreign ships through the territorial sea except in accordance with this Convention. In particular, in the application of this Convention or of any laws or regulations adopted in conformity with this Convention, the coastal State shall not:

(a) impose requirements on foreign ships which have the practical effect of denying or impairing the right of innocent passage; or

(b) discriminate in form or in fact against the ships of any State or against ships carrying cargoes to, from or on behalf of any State.

2. The coastal State shall give appropriate publicity to any danger to navigation, of which it has knowledge, within its territorial sea.

Article 25

Rights of protection of the coastal State

1. The coastal State may take the necessary steps in its territorial sea to prevent passage which is not innocent.

2. In the case of ships proceeding to internal waters or a call at a port facility outside internal waters, the coastal State also has the right to take the necessary steps to prevent any breach of the conditions to which admission of those ships to internal waters or such a call is subject.

3. The coastal State may, without discrimination in form or in fact among foreign ships, suspend temporarily in specified areas of its territorial sea the innocent passage of foreign ships if such suspension is essential for the protection of its security, including weapons exercises. Such suspension shall take effect only after having been duly published.

Article 26

Charges which may be levied upon foreign ships

1. No charge may be levied upon foreign ships by reason only of their passage through the territorial sea.

2. Charges may be levied upon a foreign ship passing through the territorial sea as payment only for specific services rendered to the ship. These charges shall be levied without discrimination.

SUBSECTION B. RULES APPLICABLE TO MERCHANT SHIPS AND GOVERNMENT SHIPS OPERATED FOR COMMERCIAL PURPOSES

Article 27

Criminal jurisdiction on board a foreign ship

1. The criminal jurisdiction of the coastal State should not be exercised on board a foreign ship passing through the territorial sea to arrest any person or to conduct any investigation in connection with any crime committed on board the ship during its passage, save only in the following cases:

(a) if the consequences of the crime extend to the coastal State;

(b) if the crime is of a kind to disturb the peace of the country or the good order of the territorial sea;

(c) if the assistance of the local authorities has been requested by the master of the ship or by a diplomatic agent or consular officer of the flag State; or

(d) if such measures are necessary for the suppression of illicit traffic in narcotic drugs or psychotropic substances.

2. The above provisions do not affect the right of the coastal State to take any steps authorized by its laws for the purpose of an arrest or investigation on board a foreign ship passing through the territorial sea after leaving internal waters.

3. In the cases provided for in paragraphs 1 and 2, the coastal State shall, if the master so requests, notify a diplomatic agent or consular officer of the flag State before taking any steps, and shall facilitate contact between such agent or officer and the ship's crew. In cases of emergency this notification may be communicated while the measures are being taken.

4. In considering whether or in what manner an arrest should be made, the local authorities shall have due regard to the interests of navigation.

5. Except as provided in Part XII or with respect to violations of laws and regulations adopted in accordance with Part V, the coastal State may not take any steps on board a foreign

ship passing through the territorial sea to arrest any person or to conduct any investigation in connection with any crime committed before the ship entered the territorial sea, if the ship, proceeding from a foreign port, is only passing through the territorial sea without entering internal waters.

Article 28

Civil jurisdiction in relation to foreign ships

1. The coastal State should not stop or divert a foreign ship passing through the territorial sea for the purpose of exercising civil jurisdiction in relation to a person on board the ship.

2. The coastal State may not levy execution against or arrest the ship for the purpose of any civil proceedings, save only in respect of obligations or liabilities assumed or incurred by the ship itself in the course or for the purpose of its voyage through the waters of the coastal State.

3. Paragraph 2 is without prejudice to the right of the coastal State, in accordance with its laws, to levy execution against or to arrest, for the purpose of any civil proceedings, a foreign ship lying in the territorial sea, or passing through the territorial sea after leaving internal waters.

SUBSECTION C. RULES APPLICABLE TO WARSHIPS AND OTHER GOVERNMENT SHIPS OPERATED FOR NON-COMMERCIAL PURPOSES

Article 29

Definition of warships

For the purposes of this Convention, "warship" means a ship belonging to the armed forces of a State bearing the external marks distinguishing such ships of its nationality, under the command of an officer duly commissioned by the government of the State and whose name appears in the appropriate service list or its equivalent, and manned by a crew which is under regular armed forces discipline.

Article 30

Non-compliance by warships with the laws and regulations of the coastal State

If any warship does not comply with the laws and regulations of the coastal State concerning passage through the territorial sea and disregards any request for compliance therewith which is made to it, the coastal State may require it to leave the territorial sea immediately.

Article 31

Responsibility of the flag State for damage caused by a warship or other government ship operated for non-commercial purposes

The flag State shall bear international responsibility for any loss or damage to the coastal State resulting from the non-compliance by a warship or other government ship operated for non-commercial purposes with the laws and regulations of the coastal State concerning passage through the territorial sea or with the provisions of this Convention or other rules of international law.

Article 32

Immunities of warships and other government ships
operated for non-commercial purposes

With such exceptions as are contained in subsection A and in articles 30 and 31, nothing in this Convention affects the immunities of warships and other government ships operated for non-commercial purposes.

SECTION 4. CONTIGUOUS ZONE

Article 33

Contiguous zone

1. In a zone contiguous to its territorial sea, described as the contiguous zone, the coastal State may exercise the control necessary to:

(a) prevent infringement of its customs, fiscal, immigration or sanitary laws and regulations within its territory or territorial sea;

(b) punish infringement of the above laws and regulations committed within its territory or territorial sea.

2. The contiguous zone may not extend beyond 24 nautical miles from the baselines from which the breadth of the territorial sea is measured.

PART III
STRAITS USED FOR INTERNATIONAL NAVIGATION

SECTION 1. GENERAL PROVISIONS

Article 34

Legal status of waters forming straits used
for international navigation

1. The régime of passage through straits used for international navigation established in this Part shall not in other respects affect the legal status of the waters forming such straits or the exercise by the States bordering the straits of their sovereignty or jurisdiction over such waters and their air space, bed and subsoil.

2. The sovereignty or jurisdiction of the States bordering the straits is exercised subject to this Part and to other rules of international law.

• • •

SECTION 2. TRANSIT PASSAGE

Article 37

Scope of this section

This section applies to straits which are used for international navigation between one part of the high seas or an exclusive economic zone and another part of the high seas or an exclusive economic zone.

Article 38

Right of transit passage

1. In straits referred to in article 37, all ships and aircraft enjoy the right of transit passage, which shall not be impeded; except that, if the strait is formed by an island of a State bordering the strait and its mainland, transit passage shall not apply if there exists seaward of the island a route through the high seas or through an exclusive economic zone of similar convenience with respect to navigational and hydrographical characteristics.

2. Transit passage means the exercise in accordance with this Part of the freedom of navigation and overflight solely for the purpose of continuous and expeditious transit of the strait between one part of the high seas or an exclusive economic zone and another part of the high seas or an exclusive economic zone. However, the requirement of continuous and expeditious transit does not preclude passage through the strait for the purpose of entering, leaving or returning from a State bordering the strait, subject to the conditions of entry to that State.

3. Any activity which is not an exercise of the right of transit passage through a strait remains subject to the other applicable provisions of this Convention.

Article 39

Duties of ships and aircraft during transit passage

1. Ships and aircraft, while exercising the right of transit passage, shall:

   (a) proceed without delay through or over the strait;

   (b) refrain from any threat or use of force against the sovereignty, territorial integrity or political independence of States bordering the strait, or in any other manner in violation of the principles of international law embodied in the Charter of the United Nations;

   (c) refrain from any activities other than those incident to their normal modes of continuous and expeditious transit unless rendered necessary by *force majeure* or by distress;

   (d) comply with other relevant provisions of this Part.

2. Ships in transit passage shall:

   (a) comply with generally accepted international regulations, procedures and practices for safety at sea, including the International Regulations for Preventing Collisions at Sea;

   (b) comply with generally accepted international regulations, procedures and practices for the prevention, reduction and control of pollution from ships.

3. Aircraft in transit passage shall:

   (a) observe the Rules of the Air established by the International Civil Aviation Organization as they apply to civil aircraft; state aircraft will normally comply with such safety measures and will at all times operate with due regard for the safety of navigation;

   (b) at all times monitor the radio frequency assigned by the competent internationally designated air traffic control authority or the appropriate international distress radio frequency.

Article 40

Research and survey activities

During transit passage, foreign ships, including marine scientific research and hydrographic survey ships, may not carry out any research or survey activities without the prior authorization of the States bordering straits.

Article 41

Sea lanes and traffic separation schemes in straits used for international navigation

1. In conformity with this Part, States bordering straits may designate sea lanes and prescribe traffic separation schemes for navigation in straits where necessary to promote the safe passage of ships.

2. Such States may, when circumstances require, and after giving due publicity thereto, substitute other sea lanes or traffic separation schemes for any sea lanes or traffic separation schemes previously designated or prescribed by them.

3. Such sea lanes and traffic separation schemes shall conform to generally accepted international regulations.

4. Before designating or substituting sea lanes or prescribing or substituting traffic separation schemes, States bordering straits shall refer proposals to the competent international organization with a view to their adoption. The organization may adopt only such sea lanes and traffic separation schemes as may be agreed with the States bordering the straits, after which the States may designate, prescribe or substitute them.

5. In respect of a strait where sea lanes or traffic separation schemes through the waters of two or more States bordering the strait are being proposed, the States concerned shall co-operate in formulating proposals in consultation with the competent international organization.

6. States bordering straits shall clearly indicate all sea lanes and traffic separation schemes designated or prescribed by them on charts to which due publicity shall be given.

7. Ships in transit passage shall respect applicable sea lanes and traffic separation schemes established in accordance with this article.

Article 42

Laws and regulations of States bordering straits relating to transit passage

1. Subject to the provisions of this section, States bordering straits may adopt laws and regulations relating to transit passage through straits, in respect of all or any of the following:

(a) the safety of navigation and the regulation of maritime traffic, as provided in article 41;

(b) the prevention, reduction and control of pollution, by giving effect to applicable international regulations regarding the discharge of oil, oily wastes and other noxious substances in the strait;

(c) with respect to fishing vessels, the prevention of fishing, including the stowage of fishing gear;

(d) the loading or unloading of any commodity, currency or person in contravention of the customs, fiscal, immigration or sanitary laws and regulations of States bordering straits.

2. Such laws and regulations shall not discriminate in form or in fact among foreign ships or in their application have the practical effect of denying, hampering or impairing the right of transit passage as defined in this section.

3. States bordering straits shall give due publicity to all such laws and regulations.

4. Foreign ships exercising the right of transit passage shall comply with such laws and regulations.

5. The flag State of a ship or the State of registry of an aircraft entitled to sovereign immunity which acts in a manner contrary to such laws and regulations or other provisions of this Part shall bear international responsibility for any loss or damage which results to States bordering straits.

Article 43

Navigational and safety aids and other improvements and
the prevention, reduction and control of pollution

User States and States bordering a strait should by agreement co-operate:

(a) in the establishment and maintenance in a strait of necessary navigational and safety aids or other improvements in aid of international navigation; and

(b) for the prevention, reduction and control of pollution from ships.

Article 44

Duties of States bordering straits

States bordering straits shall not hamper transit passage and shall give appropriate publicity to any danger to navigation or overflight within or over the strait of which they have knowledge. There shall be no suspension of transit passage.

SECTION 3. INNOCENT PASSAGE

Article 45

Innocent passage

1. The régime of innocent passage, in accordance with Part II, section 3, shall apply in straits used for international navigation:

(a) excluded from the application of the régime of transit passage under article 38, paragraph 1; or

(b) between a part of the high seas or an exclusive economic zone and the territorial sea of a foreign State.

2. There shall be no suspension of innocent passage through such straits.

PART IV
ARCHIPELAGIC STATES

Article 46

Use of terms

For the purposes of this Convention:

(a) "archipelagic State" means a State constituted wholly by one or more archipelagos and may include other islands;

(b) "archipelago" means a group of islands, including parts of islands, interconnecting waters and other natural features which are so closely interrelated that such islands, waters and other natural features form an intrinsic geographical, economic and political entity, or which historically have been regarded as such.

Article 47

Archipelagic baselines

1. An archipelagic State may draw straight archipelagic baselines joining the outermost points of the outermost islands and drying reefs of the archipelago provided that within such baselines are included the main islands and an area in which the ratio of the area of the water to the area of the land, including atolls, is between 1 to 1 and 9 to 1.

2. The length of such baselines shall not exceed 100 nautical miles, except that up to 3 per cent of the total number of baselines enclosing any archipelago may exceed that length, up to a maximum length of 125 nautical miles.

3. The drawing of such baselines shall not depart to any appreciable extent from the general configuration of the archipelago.

4. Such baselines shall not be drawn to and from low-tide elevations, unless lighthouses or similar installations which are permanently above sea level have been built on them or where a low-tide elevation is situated wholly or partly at a distance not exceeding the breadth of the territorial sea from the nearest island.

5. The system of such baselines shall not be applied by an archipelagic State in such a manner as to cut off from the high seas or the exclusive economic zone the territorial sea of another State.

6. If a part of the archipelagic waters of an archipelagic State lies between two parts of an immediately adjacent neighbouring State, existing rights and all other legitimate interests which the latter State has traditionally exercised in such waters and all rights stipulated by agreement between those States shall continue and be respected.

7. For the purpose of computing the ratio of water to land under paragraph 1, land areas may include waters lying within the fringing reefs of islands and atolls, including that part of a steep-sided oceanic plateau which is enclosed or nearly enclosed by a chain of limestone islands and drying reefs lying on the perimeter of the plateau.

8. The baselines drawn in accordance with this article shall be shown on charts of a scale or scales adequate for ascertaining their position. Alternatively, lists of geographical co-ordinates of points, specifying the geodetic datum, may be substituted.

9. The archipelagic State shall give due publicity to such charts or lists of geographical co-ordinates and shall deposit a copy of each such chart or list with the Secretary-General of the United Nations.

Article 48

Measurement of the breadth of the territorial sea, the contiguous zone,
the exclusive economic zone and the continental shelf

The breadth of the territorial sea, the contiguous zone, the exclusive economic zone and the continental shelf shall be measured from archipelagic baselines drawn in accordance with article 47.

Article 49

Legal status of archipelagic waters, of the air space over
archipelagic waters and of their bed and subsoil

1. The sovereignty of an archipelagic State extends to the waters enclosed by the archipelagic baselines drawn in accordance with article 47, described as archipelagic waters,

regardless of their depth or distance from the coast.

2. This sovereignty extends to the air space over the archipelagic waters, as well as to their bed and subsoil, and the resources contained therein.

3. This sovereignty is exercised subject to this Part.

4. The régime of archipelagic sea lanes passage established in this Part shall not in other respects affect the status of the archipelagic waters, including the sea lanes, or the exercise by the archipelagic State of its sovereignty over such waters and their air space, bed and subsoil, and the resources contained therein.

• • •

Article 51

Existing agreements, traditional fishing rights and existing submarine cables

1. Without prejudice to article 49, an archipelagic State shall respect existing agreements with other States and shall recognize traditional fishing rights and other legitimate activities of the immediately adjacent neighbouring States in certain areas falling within archipelagic waters. The terms and conditions for the exercise of such rights and activities, including the nature, the extent and the areas to which they apply, shall, at the request of any of the States concerned, be regulated by bilateral agreements between them. Such rights shall not be transferred to or shared with third States or their nationals.

2. An archipelagic State shall respect existing submarine cables laid by other States and passing through its waters without making a landfall. An archipelagic State shall permit the maintenance and replacement of such cables upon receiving due notice of their location and the intention to repair or replace them.

• • •

PART V
EXCLUSIVE ECONOMIC ZONE

Article 55

Specific legal régime of the exclusive economic zone

The exclusive economic zone is an area beyond and adjacent to the territorial sea, subject to the specific legal régime established in this Part, under which the rights and jurisdiction of the coastal State and the rights and freedoms of other States are governed by the relevant provisions of this Convention.

Article 56

Rights, jurisdiction and duties of the coastal State in the exclusive economic zone

1. In the exclusive economic zone, the coastal State has:

(a) sovereign rights for the purpose of exploring and exploiting, conserving and managing the natural resources, whether living or non-living, of the waters superjacent to the sea-bed and of the sea-bed and its subsoil, and with regard to other activities for the economic exploitation and exploration of the zone, such as the production of energy from the water, currents and winds;

(b) jurisdiction as provided for in the relevant provisions of this Convention with regard to:

    (i) the establishment and use of artificial islands, installations and structures;

    (ii) marine scientific research;

    (iii) the protection and preservation of the marine environment;

    (c) other rights and duties provided for in this Convention.

2. In exercising its rights and performing its duties under this Convention in the exclusive economic zone, the coastal State shall have due regard to the rights and duties of other States and shall act in a manner compatible with the provisions of this Convention.

3. The rights set out in this article with respect to the sea-bed and subsoil shall be exercised in accordance with Part VI.

Article 57

Breadth of the exclusive economic zone

The exclusive economic zone shall not extend beyond 200 nautical miles from the baselines from which the breadth of the territorial sea is measured.

Article 58

Rights and duties of other States in the exclusive economic zone

1. In the exclusive economic zone, all States, whether coastal or land-locked, enjoy, subject to the relevant provisions of this Convention, the freedoms referred to in article 87 of navigation and overflight and of the laying of submarine cables and pipelines, and other internationally lawful uses of the sea related to these freedoms, such as those associated with the operation of ships, aircraft and submarine cables and pipelines, and compatible with the other provisions of this Convention.

2. Articles 88 to 115 and other pertinent rules of international law apply to the exclusive economic zone in so far as they are not incompatible with this Part.

3. In exercising their rights and performing their duties under this Convention in the exclusive economic zone, States shall have due regard to the rights and duties of the coastal State and shall comply with the laws and regulations adopted by the coastal State in accordance with the provisions of this Convention and other rules of international law in so far as they are not incompatible with this Part.

Article 59

Basis for the resolution of conflicts regarding the attribution
of rights and jurisdiction in the exclusive economic zone

In cases where this Convention does not attribute rights or jurisdiction to the coastal State or to other States within the exclusive economic zone, and a conflict arises between the interests of the coastal State and any other State or States, the conflict should be resolved on the basis of equity and in the light of all the relevant circumstances, taking into account the respective importance of the interests involved to the parties as well as to the international community as a whole.

Article 60

Artificial islands, installations and structures in the exclusive economic zone

1. In the exclusive economic zone, the coastal State shall have the exclusive right to construct and to authorize and regulate the construction, operation and use of:

(a) artificial islands;

(b) installations and structures for the purposes provided for in article 56 and other economic purposes;

(c) installations and structures which may interfere with the exercise of the rights of the coastal State in the zone.

2. The coastal State shall have exclusive jurisdiction over such artificial islands, installations and structures, including jurisdiction with regard to customs, fiscal, health, safety and immigration laws and regulations.

3. Due notice must be given of the construction of such artificial islands, installations or structures, and permanent means for giving warning of their presence must be maintained. Any installations or structures which are abandoned or disused shall be removed to ensure safety of navigation, taking into account any generally accepted international standards established in this regard by the competent international organization. Such removal shall also have due regard to fishing, the protection of the marine environment and the rights and duties of other States. Appropriate publicity shall be given to the depth, position and dimensions of any installations or structures not entirely removed.

4. The coastal State may, where necessary, establish reasonable safety zones around such artificial islands, installations and structures in which it may take appropriate measures to ensure the safety both of navigation and of the artificial islands, installations and structures.

5. The breadth of the safety zones shall be determined by the coastal State, taking into account applicable international standards. Such zones shall be designed to ensure that they are reasonably related to the nature and function of the artificial islands, installations or structures, and shall not exceed a distance of 500 metres around them, measured from each point of their outer edge, except as authorized by generally accepted international standards or as recommended by the competent international organization. Due notice shall be given of the extent of safety zones.

6. All ships must respect these safety zones and shall comply with generally accepted international standards regarding navigation in the vicinity of artificial islands, installations, structures and safety zones.

7. Artificial islands, installations and structures and the safety zones around them may not be established where interference may be caused to the use of recognized sea lanes essential to international navigation.

8. Artificial islands, installations and structures do not possess the status of islands. They have no territorial sea of their own, and their presence does not affect the delimitation of the territorial sea, the exclusive economic zone or the continental shelf.

Article 61

Conservation of the living resources

1. The coastal State shall determine the allowable catch of the living resources in its exclusive economic zone.

2. The coastal State, taking into account the best scientific evidence available to it, shall ensure through proper conservation and management measures that the maintenance of the living resources in the exclusive economic zone is not endangered by over-exploitation. As appropriate, the coastal State and competent international organizations, whether subregional, regional or global, shall co-operate to this end.

3. Such measures shall also be designed to maintain or restore populations of harvested species at levels which can produce the maximum sustainable yield, as qualified by relevant environmental and economic factors, including the economic needs of coastal fishing communities and the special requirements of developing States, and taking into account fishing patterns, the interdependence of stocks and any generally recommended international minimum standards, whether subregional, regional or global.

4. In taking such measures the coastal State shall take into consideration the effects on species associated with or dependent upon harvested species with a view to maintaining or restoring populations of such associated or dependent species above levels at which their reproduction may become seriously threatened.

5. Available scientific information, catch and fishing effort statistics, and other data relevant to the conservation of fish stocks shall be contributed and exchanged on a regular basis through competent international organizations, whether subregional, regional or global, where appropriate and with participation by all States concerned, including States whose nationals are allowed to fish in the exclusive economic zone.

Article 62

Utilization of the living resources

1. The coastal State shall promote the objective of optimum utilization of the living resources in the exclusive economic zone without prejudice to article 61.

2. The coastal State shall determine its capability to harvest the living resources of the exclusive economic zone. Where the coastal State does not have the capacity to harvest the entire allowable catch, it shall, through agreements or other arrangements and pursuant to the terms, conditions, laws and regulations referred to in paragraph 4, give other States access to the surplus of the allowable catch, having particular regard to the provisions of articles 69 and 70, especially in relation to the developing States mentioned therein.

3. In giving access to other States to its exclusive economic zone under this article, the coastal State shall take into account all relevant factors, including, *inter alia*, the significance of the living resources of the area to the economy of the coastal State concerned and its other national interests, the provisions of articles 69 and 70, the requirements of developing States in the subregion or region in harvesting part of the surplus and the need to minimize economic dislocation in States whose nationals have habitually fished in the zone or which have made substantial efforts in research and identification of stocks.

4. Nationals of other States fishing in the exclusive economic zone shall comply with the conservation measures and with the other terms and conditions established in the laws and regulations of the coastal State. These laws and regulations shall be consistent with this Convention and may relate, *inter alia*, to the following:

(a) licensing of fishermen, fishing vessels and equipment, including payment of fees and other forms of remuneration, which, in the case of developing coastal States, may consist of adequate compensation in the field of financing, equipment and technology relating to the fishing industry;

(b) determining the species which may be caught, and fixing quotas of catch, whether in relation to particular stocks or groups of stocks or catch per vessel over a period of time or to the catch by nationals of any State during a specified period;

(c) regulating seasons and areas of fishing, the types, sizes and amount of gear, and the types, sizes and number of fishing vessels that may be used;

(d) fixing the age and size of fish and other species that may be caught;

(e) specifying information required of fishing vessels, including catch and effort statistics and vessel position reports;

(f) requiring, under the authorization and control of the coastal State, the conduct of specified fisheries research programmes and regulating the conduct of such research, including the sampling of catches, disposition of samples and reporting of associated scientific data;

(g) the placing of observers or trainees on board such vessels by the coastal State;

(h) the landing of all or any part of the catch by such vessels in the ports of the coastal State;

(i) terms and conditions relating to joint ventures or other co-operative arrangements;

(j) requirements for the training of personnel and the transfer of fisheries technology, including enhancement of the coastal State's capacity of undertaking fisheries research;

(k) enforcement procedures.

5. Coastal States shall give due notice of conservation and management laws and regulations.

Article 63

Stocks occurring within the exclusive economic zones of two or more coastal States or both within the exclusive economic zone and in an area beyond and adjacent to it

1. Where the same stock or stocks of associated species occur within the exclusive economic zones of two or more coastal States, these States shall seek, either directly or through appropriate subregional or regional organizations, to agree upon the measures necessary to co-ordinate and ensure the conservation and development of such stocks without prejudice to the other provisions of this Part.

2. Where the same stock or stocks of associated species occur both within the exclusive economic zone and in an area beyond and adjacent to the zone, the coastal State and the States fishing for such stocks in the adjacent area shall seek, either directly or through appropriate subregional or regional organizations, to agree upon the measures necessary for the conservation of these stocks in the adjacent area.

Article 64

Highly migratory species

1. The coastal State and other States whose nationals fish in the region for the highly migratory species listed in Annex I shall co-operate directly or through appropriate international organizations with a view to ensuring conservation and promoting the objective of optimum utilization of such species throughout the region, both within and beyond the

exclusive economic zone. In regions for which no appropriate international organization exists, the coastal State and other States whose nationals harvest these species in the region shall co-operate to establish such an organization and participate in its work.

2. The provisions of paragraph 1 apply in addition to the other provisions of this Part.

Article 65

Marine mammals

Nothing in this Part restricts the right of a coastal State or the competence of an international organization, as appropriate, to prohibit, limit or regulate the exploitation of marine mammals more strictly than provided for in this Part. States shall co-operate with a view to the conservation of marine mammals and in the case of cetaceans shall in particular work through the appropriate international organizations for their conservation, management and study.

Article 66

Anadromous stocks

1. States in whose rivers anadromous stocks originate shall have the primary interest in and responsibility for such stocks.

2. The State of origin of anadromous stocks shall ensure their conservation by the establishment of appropriate regulatory measures for fishing in all waters landward of the outer limits of its exclusive economic zone and for fishing provided for in paragraph 3(b). The State of origin may, after consultations with the other States referred to in paragraphs 3 and 4 fishing these stocks, establish total allowable catches for stocks originating in its rivers.

3. (a) Fisheries for anadromous stocks shall be conducted only in waters landward of the outer limits of exclusive economic zones, except in cases where this provision would result in economic dislocation for a State other than the State of origin. With respect to such fishing beyond the outer limits of the exclusive economic zone, States concerned shall maintain consultations with a view to achieving agreement on terms and conditions of such fishing giving due regard to the conservation requirements and the needs of the State of origin in respect of these stocks.

(b) The State of origin shall co-operate in minimizing economic dislocation in such other States fishing these stocks, taking into account the normal catch and the mode of operations of such States, and all the areas in which such fishing has occurred.

(c) States referred to in subparagraph (b), participating by agreement with the State of origin in measures to renew anadromous stocks, particularly by expenditures for that purpose, shall be given special consideration by the State of origin in the harvesting of stocks originating in its rivers.

(d) Enforcement of regulations regarding anadromous stocks beyond the exclusive economic zone shall be by agreement between the State of origin and the other States concerned.

4. In cases where anadromous stocks migrate into or through the waters landward of the outer limits of the exclusive economic zone of a State other than the State of origin, such State shall co-operate with the State of origin with regard to the conservation and management of such stocks.

5. The State of origin of anadromous stocks and other States fishing these stocks shall make arrangements for the implementation of the provisions of this article, where appropriate, through regional organizations.

Article 67

Catadromous species

1. A coastal State in whose waters catadromous species spend the greater part of their life cycle shall have responsibility for the management of these species and shall ensure the ingress and egress of migrating fish.

2. Harvesting of catadromous species shall be conducted only in waters landward of the outer limits of exclusive economic zones. When conducted in exclusive economic zones, harvesting shall be subject to this article and the other provisions of this Convention concerning fishing in these zones.

3. In cases where catadromous fish migrate through the exclusive economic zone of another State, whether as juvenile or maturing fish, the management, including harvesting, of such fish shall be regulated by agreement between the State mentioned in paragraph 1 and the other State concerned. Such agreement shall ensure the rational management of the species and take into account the responsibilities of the State mentioned in paragraph 1 for the maintenance of these species.

• • •

Article 73

Enforcement of laws and regulations of the coastal State

1. The coastal State may, in the exercise of its sovereign rights to explore, exploit, conserve and manage the living resources in the exclusive economic zone, take such measures, including boarding, inspection, arrest and judicial proceedings, as may be necessary to ensure compliance with the laws and regulations adopted by it in conformity with this Convention.

2. Arrested vessels and their crews shall be promptly released upon the posting of reasonable bond or other security.

3. Coastal State penalties for violations of fisheries laws and regulations in the exclusive economic zone may not include imprisonment, in the absence of agreements to the contrary by the States concerned, or any other form of corporal punishment.

4. In cases of arrest or detention of foreign vessels the coastal State shall promptly notify the flag State, through appropriate channels, of the action taken and of any penalties subsequently imposed.

Article 74

Delimitation of the exclusive economic zone between
States with opposite or adjacent coasts

1. The delimitation of the exclusive economic zone between States with opposite or adjacent coasts shall be effected by agreement on the basis of international law, as referred to in Article 38 of the Statute of the International Court of Justice, in order to achieve an equitable solution.

2. If no agreement can be reached within a reasonable period of time, the States concerned shall resort to the procedures provided for in Part XV.

3. Pending agreement as provided for in paragraph 1, the States concerned, in a spirit of understanding and co-operation, shall make every effort to enter into provisional arrangements of a practical nature and, during this transitional period, not to jeopardize or hamper the reaching of the final agreement. Such arrangements shall be without prejudice to the final delimitation.

4. Where there is an agreement in force between the States concerned, questions relating to the delimitation of the exclusive economic zone shall be determined in accordance with the provisions of that agreement.

• • •

PART VI
CONTINENTAL SHELF

Article 76

Definition of the continental shelf

1. The continental shelf of a coastal State comprises the sea-bed and subsoil of the submarine areas that extend beyond its territorial sea throughout the natural prolongation of its land territory to the outer edge of the continental margin, or to a distance of 200 nautical miles from the baselines from which the breadth of the territorial sea is measured where the outer edge of the continental margin does not extend up to that distance.

2. The continental shelf of a coastal State shall not extend beyond the limits provided for in paragraphs 4 to 6.

3. The continental margin comprises the submerged prolongation of the land mass of the coastal State, and consists of the sea-bed and subsoil of the shelf, the slope and the rise. It does not include the deep ocean floor with its oceanic ridges or the subsoil thereof.

4. (a) For the purposes of this Convention, the coastal State shall establish the outer edge of the continental margin wherever the margin extends beyond 200 nautical miles from the baselines from which the breadth of the territorial sea is measured, by either:

(i) a line delineated in accordance with paragraph 7 by reference to the outermost fixed points at each of which the thickness of sedimentary rocks is at least 1 per cent of the shortest distance from such point to the foot of the continental slope; or

(ii) a line delineated in accordance with paragraph 7 by reference to fixed points not more than 60 nautical miles from the foot of the continental slope.

(b) In the absence of evidence to the contrary, the foot of the continental slope shall be determined as the point of maximum change in the gradient at its base.

5. The fixed points comprising the line of the outer limits of the continental shelf on the sea-bed, drawn in accordance with paragraph 4(a)(i) and (ii), either shall not exceed 350 nautical miles from the baselines from which the breadth of the territorial sea is measured or shall not exceed 100 nautical miles from the 2,500 metre isobath, which is a line connecting the depth of 2,500 metres.

6. Notwithstanding the provisions of paragraph 5, on submarine ridges, the outer limit of the continental shelf shall not exceed 350 nautical miles from the baselines from which the

breadth of the territorial sea is measured. This paragraph does not apply to submarine elevations that are natural components of the continental margin, such as its plateaux, rises, caps, banks and spurs.

7. The coastal State shall delineate the outer limits of its continental shelf, where that shelf extends beyond 200 nautical miles from the baselines from which the breadth of the territorial sea is measured, by straight lines not exceeding 60 nautical miles in length, connecting fixed points, defined by co-ordinates of latitude and longitude.

8. Information on the limits of the continental shelf beyond 200 nautical miles from the baselines from which the breadth of the territorial sea is measured shall be submitted by the coastal State to the Commission on the Limits of the Continental Shelf set up under Annex II on the basis of equitable geographical representation. The Commission shall make recommendations to coastal States on matters related to the establishment of the outer limits of their continental shelf. The limits of the shelf established by a coastal State on the basis of these recommendations shall be final and binding.

9. The coastal State shall deposit with the Secretary-General of the United Nations charts and relevant information, including geodetic data, permanently describing the outer limits of its continental shelf. The Secretary-General shall give due publicity thereto.

10. The provisions of this article are without prejudice to the question of delimitation of the continental shelf between States with opposite or adjacent coasts.

Article 77

Rights of the coastal State over the continental shelf

1. The coastal State exercises over the continental shelf sovereign rights for the purpose of exploring it and exploiting its natural resources.

2. The rights referred to in paragraph 1 are exclusive in the sense that if the coastal State does not explore the continental shelf or exploit its natural resources, no one may undertake these activities without the express consent of the coastal State.

3. The rights of the coastal State over the continental shelf do not depend on occupation, effective or notional, or on any express proclamation.

4. The natural resources referred to in this Part consist of the mineral and other non-living resources of the sea-bed and subsoil together with living organisms belonging to sedentary species, that is to say, organisms which, at the harvestable stage, either are immobile on or under the sea-bed or are unable to move except in constant physical contact with the sea-bed or the subsoil.

Article 78

Legal status of the superjacent waters and air space
and the rights and freedoms of other States

1. The rights of the coastal State over the continental shelf do not affect the legal status of the superjacent waters or of the air space above those waters.

2. The exercise of the rights of the coastal State over the continental shelf must not infringe or result in any unjustifiable interference with navigation and other rights and freedoms of other States as provided for in this Convention.

Article 79

Submarine cables and pipelines on the continental shelf

1. All States are entitled to lay submarine cables and pipelines on the continental shelf, in accordance with the provisions of this article.

2. Subject to its right to take reasonable measures for the exploration of the continental shelf, the exploitation of its natural resources and the prevention, reduction and control of pollution from pipelines, the coastal State may not impede the laying or maintenance of such cables or pipelines.

3. The delineation of the course for the laying of such pipelines on the continental shelf is subject to the consent of the coastal State.

4. Nothing in this Part affects the right of the coastal State to establish conditions for cables or pipelines entering its territory or territorial sea, or its jurisdiction over cables and pipelines constructed or used in connection with the exploration of its continental shelf or exploitation of its resources or the operations of artificial islands, installations and structures under its jurisdiction.

5. When laying submarine cables or pipelines, States shall have due regard to cables or pipelines already in position. In particular, possibilities of repairing existing cables or pipelines shall not be prejudiced.

Article 80

Artificial islands, installations and structures on the continental shelf

Article 60 applies *mutatis mutandis* to artificial islands, installations and structures on the continental shelf.

Article 81

Drilling on the continental shelf

The coastal State shall have the exclusive right to authorize and regulate drilling on the continental shelf for all purposes.

Article 82

Payments and contributions with respect to the exploitation
of the continental shelf beyond 200 nautical miles

1. The coastal State shall make payments or contributions in kind in respect of the exploitation of the non-living resources of the continental shelf beyond 200 nautical miles from the baselines from which the breadth of the territorial sea is measured.

2. The payments and contributions shall be made annually with respect to all production at a site after the first five years of production at that site. For the sixth year, the rate of payment or contribution shall be 1 per cent of the value or volume of production at the site. The rate shall increase by 1 per cent for each subsequent year until the twelfth year and shall remain at 7 per cent thereafter. Production does not include resources used in connection with exploitation.

3. A developing State which is a net importer of a mineral resource produced from its continental shelf is exempt from making such payments or contributions in respect of that mineral resource.

4. The payments or contributions shall be made through the Authority, which shall distribute them to State Parties to this Convention, on the basis of equitable sharing criteria, taking into account the interests and needs of developing States, particularly the least developed and the land-locked among them.

Article 83

Delimitation of the continental shelf between States with opposite or adjacent coasts
1. The delimitation of the continental shelf between States with opposite or adjacent coasts shall be effected by agreement on the basis of international law, as referred to in Article 38 of the Statute of the International Court of Justice, in order to achieve an equitable solution.

2. If no agreement can be reached within a reasonable period of time, the States concerned shall resort to the procedures provided for in Part XV.

3. Pending agreement as provided for in paragraph 1, the States concerned, in a spirit of understanding and co-operation, shall make every effort to enter into provisional arrangements of a practical nature and, during this transitional period, not to jeopardize or hamper the reaching of the final agreement. Such arrangements shall be without prejudice to the final delimitation.

4. Where there is an agreement in force between the States concerned, questions relating to the delimitation of the continental shelf shall be determined in accordance with the provisions of that agreement.

• • •

PART VII
HIGH SEAS

SECTION 1. GENERAL PROVISIONS

Article 86

Application of the provisions of this Part
The provisions of this Part apply to all parts of the sea that are not included in the exclusive economic zone, in the territorial sea or in the internal waters of a State, or in the archipelagic waters of an archipelagic State. This article does not entail any abridgement of the freedoms enjoyed by all States in the exclusive economic zone in accordance with article 58.

Article 87

Freedom of the high seas
1. The high seas are open to all States, whether coastal or land-locked. Freedom of the high seas is exercised under the conditions laid down by this Convention and by other rules of international law. It comprises, *inter alia*, both for coastal and land-locked States:
  (a) freedom of navigation;
  (b) freedom of overflight;
  (c) freedom to lay submarine cables and pipelines, subject to Part VI;

(d) freedom to construct artificial islands and other installations permitted under international law, subject to Part VI;

(e) freedom of fishing, subject to the conditions laid down in section 2;

(f) freedom of scientific research, subject to Parts VI and XIII.

2. These freedoms shall be exercised by all States with due regard for the interests of other States in their exercise of the freedom of the high seas, and also with due regard for the rights under this Convention with respect to activities in the Area.

Article 88

Reservation of the high seas for peaceful purposes

The high seas shall be reserved for peaceful purposes.

Article 89

Invalidity of claims of sovereignty over the high seas

No State may validly purport to subject any part of the high seas to its sovereignty.

Article 90

Right of navigation

Every State, whether coastal or land-locked, has the right to sail ships flying its flag on the high seas.

Article 91

Nationality of ships

1. Every State shall fix the conditions for the grant of its nationality to ships, for the registration of ships in its territory, and for the right to fly its flag. Ships have the nationality of the State whose flag they are entitled to fly. There must exist a genuine link between the State and the ship.

2. Every State shall issue to ships to which it has granted the right to fly its flag documents to that effect.

Article 92

Status of ships

1. Ships shall sail under the flag of one State only and, save in exceptional cases expressly provided for in international treaties or in this Convention, shall be subject to its exclusive jurisdiction on the high seas. A ship may not change its flag during a voyage or while in a port of call, save in the case of a real transfer of ownership or change of registry.

2. A ship which sails under the flags of two or more States, using them according to convenience, may not claim any of the nationalities in question with respect to any other State, and may be assimilated to a ship without nationality.

Article 93

*Ships flying the flag of the United Nations, its specialized agencies
and the International Atomic Energy Agency*

The preceding articles do not prejudice the question of ships employed on the official service of the United Nations, its specialized agencies or the International Atomic Energy Agency, flying the flag of the organization.

Article 94

Duties of the flag State

1. Every State shall effectively exercise its jurisdiction and control in administrative, technical and social matters over ships flying its flag.

2. In particular every State shall:

(a) maintain a register of ships containing the names and particulars of ships flying its flag, except those which are excluded from generally accepted international regulations on account of their small size; and

(b) assume jurisdiction under its internal law over each ship flying its flag and its master, officers and crew in respect of administrative, technical and social matters concerning the ship.

3. Every State shall take such measures for ships flying its flag as are necessary to ensure safety at sea with regard, *inter alia*, to:

(a) the construction, equipment and seaworthiness of ships;

(b) the manning of ships, labour conditions and the training of crews, taking into account the applicable international instruments;

(c) the use of signals, the maintenance of communications and the prevention of collisions.

4. Such measures shall include those necessary to ensure:

(a) that each ship, before registration and thereafter at appropriate intervals, is surveyed by a qualified surveyor of ships, and has on board such charts, nautical publications and navigational equipment and instruments as are appropriate for the safe navigation of the ship;

(b) that each ship is in the charge of a master and officers who possess appropriate qualifications, in particular, in seamanship, navigation, communications and marine engineering, and that the crew is appropriate in qualification and numbers for the type, size, machinery and equipment of the ship;

(c) that the master, officers and, to the extent appropriate, the crew are fully conversant with and required to observe the applicable international regulations concerning the safety of life at sea, the prevention of collisions, the prevention, reduction and control of marine pollution, and the maintenance of communications by radio.

5. In taking the measures called for in paragraphs 3 and 4 each State is required to conform to generally accepted international regulations, procedures and practices and to take any steps which may be necessary to secure their observance.

6. A State which has clear grounds to believe that proper jurisdiction and control with respect to a ship have not been exercised may report the facts to the flag State. Upon receiving

such a report, the flag State shall investigate the matter and, if appropriate, take any action necessary to remedy the situation.

7. Each State shall cause an inquiry to be held by or before a suitably qualified person or persons into every marine casualty or incident of navigation on the high seas involving a ship flying its flag and causing loss of life or serious injury to nationals of another State or serious damage to ships or installations of another State or to the marine environment. The flag State and the other State shall co-operate in the conduct of any inquiry held by that other State into any such marine casualty or incident of navigation.

Article 95

Immunity of warships on the high seas

Warships on the high seas have complete immunity from the jurisdiction of any State other than the flag State.

Article 96

Immunity of ships used only on government non-commercial service

Ships owned or operated by a State and used only on government non-commercial service shall, on the high seas, have complete immunity from the jurisdiction of any State other than the flag State.

Article 97

Penal jurisdiction in matters of collision or any other incident of navigation

1. In the event of a collision or any other incident of navigation concerning a ship on the high seas, involving the penal or disciplinary responsibility of the master or of any other person in the service of the ship, no penal or disciplinary proceedings may be instituted against such person except before the judicial or administrative authorities either of the flag State or of the State of which such person is a national.

2. In disciplinary matters, the State which has issued a master's certificate or a certificate of competence or licence shall alone be competent, after due legal process, to pronounce the withdrawal of such certificates, even if the holder is not a national of the State which issued them.

3. No arrest or detention of the ship, even as a measure of investigation, shall be ordered by any authorities other than those of the flag State.

Article 98

Duty to render assistance

1. Every State shall require the master of a ship flying its flag, in so far as he can do so without serious danger to the ship, the crew or the passengers:

(a) to render assistance to any person found at sea in danger of being lost;

(b) to proceed with all possible speed to the rescue of persons in distress, if informed of their need of assistance, in so far as such action may reasonably be expected of him;

(c) after a collision, to render assistance to the other ship, its crew and its passengers and, where possible, to inform the other ship of the name of his own ship, its port of registry and the nearest port at which it will call.

2. Every coastal State shall promote the establishment, operation and maintenance of an adequate and effective search and rescue service regarding safety on and over the sea and, where circumstances so require, by way of mutual regional arrangements co-operate with neighbouring States for this purpose.

Article 99

Prohibition of the transport of slaves

Every State shall take effective measures to prevent and punish the transport of slaves in ships authorized to fly its flag and to prevent the unlawful use of its flag for that purpose. Any slave taking refuge on board any ship, whatever its flag, shall *ipso facto* be free.

Article 100

Duty to co-operate in the repression of piracy

All States shall co-operate to the fullest possible extent in the repression of piracy on the high seas or in any other place outside the jurisdiction of any State.

Article 101

Definition of piracy

Piracy consists of any of the following acts:

(a) any illegal acts of violence or detention, or any act of depredation, committed for private ends by the crew or the passengers of a private ship or a private aircraft, and directed:

(i) on the high seas, against another ship or aircraft, or against persons or property on board such ships or aircraft;

(ii) against a ship, aircraft, persons or property in a place outside the jurisdiction of any State;

(b) any act of voluntary participation in the operation of a ship or of an aircraft with knowledge of facts making it a pirate-ship or aircraft;

(c) any act of inciting or of intentionally facilitating an act described in subparagraph (a) or (b).

Article 102

Piracy by a warship, government ship or government aircraft whose crew has mutinied

The acts of piracy, as defined in article 101, committed by a warship, government ship or government aircraft whose crew has mutinied and taken control of the ship or aircraft are assimilated to acts committed by a private ship or aircraft.

Article 103

Definition of a pirate ship or aircraft

A ship or aircraft is considered a pirate ship or aircraft if it is intended by the persons in dominant control to be used for the purpose of committing one of the acts referred to in article 101. The same applies if the ship or aircraft has been used to commit any such act, so long as it remains under the control of the persons guilty of that act.

Article 104

Retention or loss of the nationality of a pirate ship or aircraft

A ship or aircraft may retain its nationality although it has become a pirate ship or aircraft. The retention or loss of nationality is determined by the law of the State from which such nationality was derived.

Article 105

Seizure of a pirate ship or aircraft

On the high seas, or in any other place outside the jurisdiction of any State, every State may seize a pirate ship or aircraft, or a ship or aircraft taken by piracy and under the control of pirates, and arrest the persons and seize the property on board. The courts of the State which carried out the seizure may decide upon the penalties to be imposed, and may also determine the action to be taken with regard to the ships, aircraft or property, subject to the rights of third parties acting in good faith.

Article 106

Liability for seizure without adequate grounds

Where the seizure of a ship or aircraft on suspicion of piracy has been effected without adequate grounds, the State making the seizure shall be liable to the State the nationality of which is possessed by the ship or aircraft for any loss or damage caused by the seizure.

Article 107

Ships and aircraft which are entitled to seize on account of piracy

A seizure on account of piracy may be carried out only by warships or military aircraft, or other ships or aircraft clearly marked and identifiable as being on government service and authorized to that effect.

Article 108

Illicit traffic in narcotic drugs or psychotropic substances

1. All States shall co-operate in the suppression of illicit traffic in narcotic drugs and psychotropic substances engaged in by ships on the high seas contrary to international conventions.

2. Any State which has reasonable grounds for believing that a ship flying its flag is engaged in illicit traffic in narcotic drugs or psychotropic substances may request the co-operation of other States to suppress such traffic.

Article 109

Unauthorized broadcasting from the high seas

1. All States shall co-operate in the suppression of unauthorized broadcasting from the high seas.

2. For the purposes of this Convention, "unauthorized broadcasting" means the transmission of sound radio or television broadcasts from a ship or installation on the high seas

intended for reception by the general public contrary to international regulations, but excluding the transmission of distress calls.

3. Any person engaged in unauthorized broadcasting may be prosecuted before the court of:

(a) the flag State of the ship;

(b) the State of registry of the installation;

(c) the State of which the person is a national;

(d) any State where the transmissions can be received; or

(e) any State where authorized radio communication is suffering interference.

4. On the high seas, a State having jurisdiction in accordance with paragraph 3 may, in conformity with article 110, arrest any person or ship engaged in unauthorized broadcasting and seize the broadcasting apparatus.

Article 110

Right of visit

1. Except where acts of interference derive from powers conferred by treaty, a warship which encounters on the high seas a foreign ship, other than a ship entitled to complete immunity in accordance with articles 95 and 96, is not justified in boarding it unless there is reasonable ground for suspecting that:

(a) the ship is engaged in piracy;

(b) the ship is engaged in the slave trade;

(c) the ship is engaged in unauthorized broadcasting and the flag State of the warship has jurisdiction under article 109;

(d) the ship is without nationality; or

(e) though flying a foreign flag or refusing to show its flag, the ship is, in reality, of the same nationality as the warship.

2. In the cases provided for in paragraph 1, the warship may proceed to verify the ship's right to fly its flag. To this end, it may send a boat under the command of an officer to the suspected ship. If suspicion remains after the documents have been checked, it may proceed to a further examination on board the ship, which must be carried out with all possible consideration.

3. If the suspicions prove to be unfounded, and provided that the ship boarded has not committed any act justifying them, it shall be compensated for any loss or damage that may have been sustained.

4. These provisions apply *mutatis mutandis* to military aircraft.

5. These provisions also apply to any other duly authorized ships or aircraft clearly marked and identifiable as being on government service.

Article 111

Right of hot pursuit

1. The hot pursuit of a foreign ship may be undertaken when the competent authorities of the coastal State have good reason to believe that the ship has violated the laws and regulations of that State. Such pursuit must be commenced when the foreign ship or one of its boats is within the internal waters, the archipelagic waters, the territorial sea or the

contiguous zone of the pursuing State, and may only be continued outside the territorial sea or the contiguous zone if the pursuit has not been interrupted. It is not necessary that, at the time when the foreign ship within the territorial sea or the contiguous zone receives the order to stop, the ship giving the order should likewise be within the territorial sea or the contiguous zone. If the foreign ship is within a contiguous zone, as defined in article 33, the pursuit may only be undertaken if there has been a violation of the rights for the protection of which the zone was established.

2. The right of hot pursuit shall apply *mutatis mutandis* to violations in the exclusive economic zone or on the continental shelf, including safety zones around continental shelf installations, of the laws and regulations of the coastal State applicable in accordance with this Convention to the exclusive economic zone or the continental shelf, including such safety zones.

3. The right of hot pursuit ceases as soon as the ship pursued enters the territorial sea of its own State or of a third State.

4. Hot pursuit is not deemed to have begun unless the pursuing ship has satisfied itself by such practicable means as may be available that the ship pursued or one of its boats or other craft working as a team and using the ship pursued as a mother ship is within the limits of the territorial sea, or, as the case may be, within the contiguous zone or the exclusive economic zone or above the continental shelf. The pursuit may only be commenced after a visual or auditory signal to stop has been given at a distance which enables it to be seen or heard by the foreign ship.

5. The right of hot pursuit may be exercised only by warships or military aircraft, or other ships or aircraft clearly marked and identifiable as being on government service and authorized to that effect.

6. Where hot pursuit is effected by an aircraft:

    (a) the provisions of paragraphs 1 to 4 shall apply *mutatis mutandis*;

    (b) the aircraft giving the order to stop must itself actively pursue the ship until a ship or another aircraft of the coastal State, summoned by the aircraft, arrives to take over the pursuit, unless the aircraft is itself able to arrest the ship. It does not suffice to justify an arrest outside the territorial sea that the ship was merely sighted by the aircraft as an offender or suspected offender, if it was not both ordered to stop and pursued by the aircraft itself or other aircraft or ships which continue the pursuit without interruption.

7. The release of a ship arrested within the jurisdiction of a State and escorted to a port of that State for the purposes of an inquiry before the competent authorities may not be claimed solely on the ground that the ship, in the course of its voyage, was escorted across a portion of the exclusive economic zone or the high seas, if the circumstances rendered this necessary.

8. Where a ship has been stopped or arrested outside the territorial sea in circumstances which do not justify the exercise of the right of hot pursuit, it shall be compensated for any loss or damage that may have been thereby sustained.

• • •

PART VIII
REGIME OF ISLANDS

Article 121

Régime of islands

1. An island is a naturally formed area of land, surrounded by water, which is above water at high tide.

2. Except as provided for in paragraph 3, the territorial sea, the contiguous zone, the exclusive economic zone and the continental shelf of an island are determined in accordance with the provisions of this Convention applicable to other land territory.

3. Rocks which cannot sustain human habitation or economic life of their own shall have no exclusive economic zone or continental shelf.

• • •

PART XI
THE AREA

• • •

SECTION 2. PRINCIPLES GOVERNING THE AREA

Article 136

Common heritage of mankind
The Area and its resources are the common heritage of mankind.

Article 137

Legal status of the Area and its resources

1. No State shall claim or exercise sovereignty or sovereign rights over any part of the Area or its resources, nor shall any State or natural or juridical person appropriate any part thereof. No such claim or exercise of sovereignty or sovereign rights nor such appropriation shall be recognized.

2. All rights in the resources of the Area are vested in mankind as a whole, on whose behalf the Authority shall act. These resources are not subject to alienation. The minerals recovered from the Area, however, may only be alienated in accordance with this Part and the rules, regulations and procedures of the Authority.

3. No State or natural or juridical person shall claim, acquire or exercise rights with respect to the minerals recovered from the Area except in accordance with this Part. Otherwise, no such claim, acquisition or exercise of such rights shall be recognized.

Article 138

General conduct of States in relation to the Area
The general conduct of States in relation to the Area shall be in accordance with the provisions of this Part, the principles embodied in the Charter of the United Nations and other rules of

international law in the interests of maintaining peace and security and promoting international co-operation and mutual understanding.

Article 139

Responsibility to ensure compliance and liability for damage

1. States Parties shall have the responsibility to ensure that activities in the Area, whether carried out by States Parties, or state enterprises or natural or juridical persons which possess the nationality of States Parties or are effectively controlled by them or their nationals, shall be carried out in conformity with this Part. The same responsibility applies to international organizations for activities in the Area carried out by such organizations.

2. Without prejudice to the rules of international law and Annex III, article 22, damage caused by the failure of a State Party or international organization to carry out its responsibilities under this Part shall entail liability; States Parties or international organizations acting together shall bear joint and several liability. A State Party shall not however be liable for damage caused by any failure to comply with this Part by a person whom it has sponsored under article 153, paragraph 2(b), if the State Party has taken all necessary and appropriate measures to secure effective compliance under article 153, paragraph 4, and Annex III, article 4, paragraph 4.

3. States Parties that are members of international organizations shall take appropriate measures to ensure the implementation of this article with respect to such organizations.

Article 140

Benefit of mankind

1. Activities in the Area shall, as specifically provided for in this Part, be carried out for the benefit of mankind as a whole, irrespective of the geographical location of States, whether coastal or land-locked, and taking into particular consideration the interests and needs of developing States and of peoples who have not attained full independence or other self-governing status recognized by the United Nations in accordance with General Assembly resolution 1514 (XV) and other relevant General Assembly resolutions.

2. The Authority shall provide for the equitable sharing of financial and other economic benefits derived from activities in the Area through any appropriate mechanism, on a non-discriminatory basis, in accordance with article 160, paragraph 2(f)(i).

Article 141

Use of the Area exclusively for peaceful purposes

The Area shall be open to use exclusively for peaceful purposes by all States, whether coastal or land-locked, without discrimination and without prejudice to the other provisions of this Part.

Article 142

Rights and legitimate interests of coastal States

1. Activities in the Area, with respect to resource deposits in the Area which lie across limits of national jurisdiction, shall be conducted with due regard to the rights and legitimate interests of any coastal State across whose jurisdiction such deposits lie.

2. Consultations, including a system of prior notification, shall be maintained with the State concerned, with a view to avoiding infringement of such rights and interests. In cases where activities in the Area may result in the exploitation of resources lying within national jurisdiction, the prior consent of the coastal State concerned shall be required.

3. Neither this Part nor any rights granted or exercised pursuant thereto shall affect the rights of coastal States to take such measures consistent with the relevant provisions of Part XII as may be necessary to prevent, mitigate or eliminate grave and imminent danger to their coastline, or related interests from pollution or threat thereof or from other hazardous occurrences resulting from or caused by any activities in the Area.

· · ·

SECTION 3. DEVELOPMENT OF RESOURCES OF THE AREA

Article 150

Policies relating to activities in the Area

Activities in the Area shall, as specifically provided for in this Part, be carried out in such a manner as to foster healthy development of the world economy and balanced growth of international trade, and to promote international co-operation for the over-all development of all countries, especially developing States, and with a view to ensuring:

(a) the development of the resources of the Area;

(b) orderly, safe and rational management of the resources of the Area, including the efficient conduct of activities in the Area and, in accordance with sound principles of conservation, the avoidance of unnecessary waste;

(c) the expansion of opportunities for participation in such activities consistent in particular with articles 144 and 148;

(d) participation in revenues by the Authority and the transfer of technology to the Enterprise and developing States as provided for in this Convention;

(e) increased availability of the minerals derived from the Area as needed in conjunction with minerals derived from other sources, to ensure supplies to consumers of such minerals;

(f) the promotion of just and stable prices remunerative to producers and fair to consumers for minerals derived both from the Area and from other sources, and the promotion of long-term equilibrium between supply and demand;

(g) the enhancement of opportunities for all States Parties, irrespective of their social and economic systems or geographical location, to participate in the development of the resources of the Area and the prevention of monopolization of activities in the Area;

(h) the protection of developing countries from adverse effects on their economies or on their export earnings resulting from a reduction in the price of an affected mineral, or in the volume of exports of that mineral, to the extent that such reduction is caused by activities in the Area, as provided in article 151;

(i) the development of the common heritage for the benefit of mankind as a whole; and

(j) conditions of access to markets for the imports of minerals produced from the resources of the Area and for imports of commodities produced from such minerals shall not be more favourable than the most favourable applied to imports from other sources.

Article 151

Production policies

1. (a) Without prejudice to the objectives set forth in article 150 and for the purpose of implementing subparagraph (h) of that article, the Authority, acting through existing forums or such new arrangements or agreements as may be appropriate, in which all interested parties, including both producers and consumers, participate, shall take measures necessary to promote the growth, efficiency and stability of markets for those commodities produced from the minerals derived from the Area, at prices remunerative to producers and fair to consumers. All States Parties shall co-operate to this end.

(b) The Authority shall have the right to participate in any commodity conference dealing with those commodities and in which all interested parties including both producers and consumers participate. The Authority shall have the right to become a party to any arrangement or agreement resulting from such conferences. Participation of the Authority in any organs established under those arrangements or agreements shall be in respect of production in the Area and in accordance with the relevant rules of those organs.

(c) The Authority shall carry out its obligations under the arrangements or agreements referred to in this paragraph in a manner which assures a uniform and non-discriminatory implementation in respect of all production in the Area of the minerals concerned. In doing so, the Authority shall act in a manner consistent with the terms of existing contracts and approved plans of work of the Enterprise.

2 (a) During the interim period specified in paragraph 3, commercial production shall not be undertaken pursuant to an approved plan of work until the operator has applied for and has been issued a production authorization by the Authority. Such production authorizations may not be applied for or issued more than five years prior to the planned commencement of commercial production under the plan of work unless, having regard to the nature and timing of project development, the rules, regulations and procedures of the Authority prescribe another period.

(b) In the application for the production authorization, the operator shall specify the annual quantity of nickel expected to be recovered under the approved plan of work. The application shall include a schedule of expenditures to be made by the operator after he has received the authorization which are reasonably calculated to allow him to begin commercial production on the date planned.

(c) for the purposes of subparagraphs (a) and (b), the Authority shall establish appropriate performance requirements in accordance with Annex III, article 17.

(d) The Authority shall issue a production authorization for the level of production applied for unless the sum of that level and the levels already authorized exceeds the nickel production ceiling, as calculated pursuant to paragraph 4 in the year of issuance of the authorization, during any year of planned production falling within the interim period.

(e) When issued, the production authorization and approved application shall become a part of the approved plan of work.

(f) If the operator's application for a production authorization is denied pursuant to subparagraph (d), the operator may apply again to the Authority at any time.

3. The interim period shall begin five years prior to 1 January of the year in which the earliest commercial production is planned to commence under an approved plan of work. If the earliest commercial production is delayed beyond the year originally planned, the

beginning of the interim period and the production ceiling originally calculated shall be adjusted accordingly. The interim period shall last 25 years or until the end of the Review Conference referred to in article 155 or until the day when such new arrangements or agreements as are referred to in paragraph 1 enter into force, whichever is earliest. The Authority shall resume the power provided in this article for the remainder of the interim period if the said arrangements or agreements should lapse or become ineffective for any reason whatsoever.

4. (a) The production ceiling for any year of the interim period shall be the sum of:

(i) the difference between the trend line values for nickel consumption, as calculated pursuant to subparagraph (b), for the year immediately prior to the year of the earliest commercial production and the year immediately prior to the commencement of the interim period; and

(ii) sixty per cent of the difference between the trend line values for nickel consumption, as calculated pursuant to subparagraph (b), for the year for which the production authorization is being applied for and the year immediately prior to the year of the earliest commercial production.

(b) For the purposes of subparagraph (a):

(i) trend line values used for computing the nickel production ceiling shall be those annual nickel consumption values on a trend line computed during the year in which a production authorization is issued. The trend line shall be derived from a linear regression of the logarithms of actual nickel consumption for the most recent 15-year period for which such data are available, time being the independent variable. This trend line shall be referred to as the original trend line;

(ii) if the annual rate of increase of the original trend line is less than 3 per cent, then the trend line used to determine the quantities referred to in subparagraph (a) shall instead be one passing through the original trend line at the value for the first year of the relevant 15-year period, and increasing at 3 per cent annually; provided however that the production ceiling established for any year of the interim period may not in any case exceed the difference between the original trend line value for that year and the original trend line value for the year immediately prior to the commencement of the interim period.

5. The Authority shall reserve to the Enterprise for its initial production a quantity of 38,000 metric tonnes of nickel from the available production ceiling calculated pursuant to paragraph 4.

6. (a) An operator may in any year produce less than or up to 8 per cent more than the level of annual production of minerals from polymetallic nodules specified in his production authorization, provided that the over-all amount of production shall not exceed that specified in the authorization. Any excess over 8 per cent and up to 20 per cent in any year, or any excess in the first and subsequent years following two consecutive years in which excesses occur, shall be negotiated with the Authority, which may require the operator to obtain a supplementary production authorization to cover additional production.

(b) Applications for such supplementary production authorizations shall be considered by the Authority only after all pending applications by operators who have not yet received production authorizations have been acted upon and due account has been taken of other likely applicants. The Authority shall be guided by the principle of not exceeding the total production allowed under the production ceiling in any year of the interim period. It shall not authorize the production under any plan of work of a quantity in excess of 46,500 metric tonnes of nickel per year.

7. The levels of production of other metals such as copper, cobalt and manganese extracted from the polymetallic nodules that are recovered pursuant to a production authorization should not be higher than those which would have been produced had the operator produced the maximum level of nickel from those nodules pursuant to this article. The Authority shall establish rules, regulations and procedures pursuant to Annex III, article 17, to implement this paragraph.

8. Rights and obligations relating to unfair economic practices under relevant multilateral trade agreements shall apply to the exploration for and exploitation of minerals from the Area. In the settlement of disputes arising under this provision, States Parties which are Parties to such multilateral trade agreements shall have recourse to the dispute settlement procedures of such agreements.

9. The Authority shall have the power to limit the level of production of minerals from the Area, other than minerals from polymetallic nodules, under such conditions and applying such methods as may be appropriate by adopting regulations in accordance with article 161, paragraph 8.

10. Upon the recommendation of the Council on the basis of advice from the Economic Planning Commission, the Assembly shall establish a system of compensation or take other measures of economic adjustment assistance including co-operation with specialized agencies and other international organizations to assist developing countries which suffer serious adverse effects on their export earnings or economies resulting from a reduction in the price of an affected mineral or in the volume of exports of that mineral, to the extent that such reduction is caused by activities in the Area. The Authority on request shall initiate studies on the problems of those States which are likely to be most seriously affected with a view to minimizing their difficulties and assisting them in their economic adjustment.

Article 152

Exercise of powers and functions by the Authority

1. The Authority shall avoid discrimination in the exercise of its powers and functions, including the granting of opportunities for activities in the Area.

2. Nevertheless, special consideration for developing States, including particular consideration for the land-locked and geographically disadvantaged among them, specifically provided for in this Part shall be permitted.

Article 153

System of exploration and exploitation

1. Activities in the Area shall be organized, carried out and controlled by the Authority on behalf of mankind as a whole in accordance with this article as well as other relevant provisions of this Part and the relevant Annexes, and the rules, regulations and procedures of the Authority.

2. Activities in the Area shall be carried out as prescribed in paragraph 3:

(a) by the Enterprise, and

(b) in association with the Authority by States Parties, or state enterprises or natural or juridical persons which possess the nationality of States Parties or are effectively controlled by them or their nationals, when sponsored by such States, or any group of the foregoing which meets the requirements provided in this Part and in Annex III.

3. Activities in the Area shall be carried out in accordance with a formal written plan of work drawn up in accordance with Annex III and approved by the Council after review by the Legal and Technical Commission. In the case of activities in the Area carried out as authorized by the Authority by the entities specified in paragraph 2(b), the plan of work shall, in accordance with Annex III, article 3, be in the form of a contract. Such contracts may provide for joint arrangements in accordance with Annex III, article 11.

4. The Authority shall exercise such control over activities in the Area as is necessary for the purpose of securing compliance with the relevant provisions of this Part and the Annexes relating thereto, and the rules, regulations and procedures of the Authority, and the plans of work approved in accordance with paragraph 3. States Parties shall assist the Authority by taking all measures necessary to ensure such compliance in accordance with article 139.

5. The Authority shall have the right to take at any time any measures provided for under this Part to ensure compliance with its provisions and the exercise of the functions of control and regulation assigned to it thereunder or under any contract. The Authority shall have the right to inspect all installations in the Area used in connection with activities in the Area.

6. A contract under paragraph 3 shall provide for security of tenure. Accordingly, the contract shall not be revised, suspended or terminated except in accordance with Annex III, articles 18 and 19.

• • •

PART XII
PROTECTION AND PRESERVATION OF THE MARINE ENVIRONMENT

SECTION 1. GENERAL PROVISIONS

Article 192

General obligation
States have the obligation to protect and preserve the marine environment.

Article 193

Sovereign right of States to exploit their natural resources
States have the sovereign right to exploit their natural resources pursuant to their environmental policies and in accordance with their duty to protect and preserve the marine environment.

Article 194

Measures to prevent, reduce and control pollution of the marine environment
1. States shall take, individually or jointly as appropriate, all measures consistent with this Convention that are necessary to prevent, reduce and control pollution of the marine environment from any source, using for this purpose the best practicable means at their

disposal and in accordance with their capabilities, and they shall endeavour to harmonize their policies in this connection.

2. States shall take all measures necessary to ensure that activities under their jurisdiction or control are so conducted as not tó cause damage by pollution to other States and their environment, and that pollution arising from incidents or activities under their jurisdiction or control does not spread beyond the areas where they exercise sovereign rights in accordance with this Convention.

3. The measures taken pursuant to this Part shall deal with all sources of pollution of the marine environment. These measures shall include, *inter alia*, those designed to minimize to the fullest possible extent:

(a) the release of toxic, harmful or noxious substances, especially those which are persistent, from land-based sources, from or through the atmosphere or by dumping;

(b) pollution from vessels, in particular measures for preventing accidents and dealing with emergencies, ensuring the safety of operations at sea, preventing intentional and unintentional discharges, and regulating the design, construction, equipment, operation and manning of vessels;

(c) pollution from installations and devices used in exploration or exploitation of the natural resources of the sea-bed and subsoil, in particular measures for preventing accidents and dealing with emergencies, ensuring the safety of operations at sea, and regulating the design, construction, equipment, operation and manning of such installations or devices;

(d) pollution from other installations and devices operating in the marine environment, in particular measures for preventing accidents and dealing with emergencies, ensuring the safety of operations at sea, and regulating the design, construction, equipment, operation and manning of such installations or devices.

4. In taking measures to prevent, reduce or control pollution of the marine environment, States shall refrain from unjustifiable interference with activities carried out by other States in the exercise of their rights and in pursuance of their duties in conformity with this Convention.

5. The measures taken in accordance with this Part shall include those necessary to protect and preserve rare or fragile ecosystems as well as the habitat of depleted, threatened or endangered species and other forms of marine life.

• • •

SECTION 2. GLOBAL AND REGIONAL CO-OPERATION

Article 197

Co-operation on a global or regional basis

States shall co-operate on a global basis and, as appropriate, on a regional basis, directly or through competent international organizations, in formulating and elaborating international rules, standards and recommended practices and procedures consistent with this Convention, for the protection and preservation of the marine environment, taking into account characteristic regional features.

Article 198

Notification of imminent or actual damage

When a State becomes aware of cases in which the marine environment is in imminent danger of being damaged or has been damaged by pollution, it shall immediately notify other States it deems likely to be affected by such damage, as well as the competent international organizations.

Article 199

Contingency plans against pollution

In the cases referred to in article 198, States in the area affected, in accordance with their capabilities, and the competent international organizations shall co-operate, to the extent possible, in eliminating the effects of pollution and preventing or minimizing the damage. To this end, States shall jointly develop and promote contingency plans for responding to pollution incidents in the marine environment.

Article 200

Studies, research programmes and exchange of information and data

States shall co-operate, directly or through competent international organizations, for the purpose of promoting studies, undertaking programmes of scientific research and encouraging the exchange of information and data acquired about pollution of the marine environment. They shall endeavour to participate actively in regional and global programmes to acquire knowledge for the assessment of the nature and extent of pollution, exposure to it, and its pathways, risks and remedies.

Article 201

Scientific criteria for regulations

In the light of the information and data acquired pursuant to article 200, States shall co-operate, directly or through competent international organizations, in establishing appropriate scientific criteria for the formulation and elaboration of rules, standards and recommended practices and procedures for the prevention, reduction and control of pollution of the marine environment.

• • •

SECTION 4. MONITORING AND ENVIRONMENTAL ASSESSMENT

Article 204

Monitoring of the risks or effects of pollution

1. States shall, consistent with the rights of other States, endeavour, as far as practicable, directly or through the competent international organizations, to observe, measure, evaluate and analyse, by recognized scientific methods, the risks or effects of pollution of the marine environment.

2. In particular, States shall keep under surveillance the effects of any activities which they permit or in which they engage in order to determine whether these activities are likely to pollute the marine environment.

Article 205

Publication of reports

States shall publish reports of the results obtained pursuant to article 204 or provide such reports at appropriate intervals to the competent international organizations, which should make them available to all States.

Article 206

Assessment of potential effects of activities

When States have reasonable grounds for believing that planned activities under their jurisdiction or control may cause substantial pollution of or significant and harmful changes to the marine environment, they shall, as far as practicable, assess the potential effects of such activities on the marine environment and shall communicate reports of the results of such assessments in the manner provided in article 205.

SECTION 5. INTERNATIONAL RULES AND NATIONAL LEGISLATION TO PREVENT, REDUCE AND CONTROL POLLUTION OF THE MARINE ENVIRONMENT

Article 207

Pollution from land-based sources

1. States shall adopt laws and regulations to prevent, reduce and control pollution of the marine environment from land-based sources, including rivers, estuaries, pipelines and outfall structures, taking into account internationally agreed rules, standards and recommended practices and procedures.

2. States shall take other measures as may be necessary to prevent, reduce and control such pollution.

3. States shall endeavour to harmonize their policies in this connection at the appropriate regional level.

4. States, acting especially through competent international organizations or diplomatic conference, shall endeavour to establish global and regional rules, standards and recommended practices and procedures to prevent, reduce and control pollution of the marine environment from land-based sources, taking into account characteristic regional features, the economic capacity of developing States and their need for economic development. Such rules, standards and recommended practices and procedures shall be re-examined from time to time as necessary.

5. Laws, regulations, measures, rules, standards and recommended practices and procedures referred to in paragraphs 1, 2 and 4 shall include those designed to minimize, to the fullest extent possible, the release of toxic, harmful or noxious substances, especially those which are persistent, into the marine environment.

Article 208

Pollution from sea-bed activities subject to national jurisdiction

1. Coastal States shall adopt laws and regulations to prevent, reduce and control pollution of the marine environment arising from or in connection with sea-bed activities subject to their jurisdiction and from artificial islands, installations and structures under their jurisdiction, pursuant to articles 60 and 80.

2. States shall take other measures as may be necessary to prevent, reduce and control such pollution.

3. Such laws, regulations and measures shall be no less effective than international rules, standards and recommended practices and procedures.

4. States shall endeavour to harmonize their policies in this connection at the appropriate regional level.

5. States, acting especially through competent international organizations or diplomatic conference, shall establish global and regional rules, standards and recommended practices and procedures to prevent, reduce and control pollution of the marine environment referred to in paragraph 1. Such rules, standards and recommended practices and procedures shall be re-examined from time to time as necessary.

Article 209

Pollution from activities in the Area

1. International rules, regulations and procedures shall be established in accordance with Part XI to prevent, reduce and control pollution of the marine environment from activities in the Area. Such rules, regulations and procedures shall be re-examined from time to time as necessary.

2. Subject to the relevant provisions of this section, States shall adopt laws and regulations to prevent, reduce and control pollution of the marine environment from activities in the Area undertaken by vessels, installations, structures and other devices flying their flag or of their registry or operating under their authority, as the case may be. The requirements of such laws and regulations shall be no less effective than the international rules, regulations and procedures referred to in paragraph 1.

Article 210

Pollution by dumping

1. States shall adopt laws and regulations to prevent, reduce and control pollution of the marine environment by dumping.

2. States shall take other measures as may be necessary to prevent, reduce and control such pollution.

3. Such laws, regulations and measures shall ensure that dumping is not carried out without the permission of the competent authorities of States.

4. States, acting especially through competent international organizations or diplomatic conference, shall endeavour to establish global and regional rules, standards and recommended practices and procedures to prevent, reduce and control such pollution. Such rules, standards and recommended practices and procedures shall be re-examined from time to time as necessary.

5. Dumping within the territorial sea and the exclusive economic zone or onto the continental shelf shall not be carried out without the express prior approval of the coastal State, which has the right to permit, regulate and control such dumping after due consideration of the matter with other States which by reason of their geographical situation may be adversely affected thereby.

6. National laws, regulations and measures shall be no less effective in preventing, reducing and controlling such pollution than the global rules and standards.

Article 211

Pollution from vessels

1. States, acting through the competent international organization or general diplomatic conference, shall establish international rules and standards to prevent, reduce and control pollution of the marine environment from vessels and promote the adoption, in the same manner, wherever appropriate, of routeing systems designed to minimize the threat of accidents which might cause pollution of the marine environment, including the coastline, and pollution damage to the related interests of coastal States. Such rules and standards shall, in the same manner, be re-examined from time to time as necessary.

2. States shall adopt laws and regulations for the prevention, reduction and control of pollution of the marine environment from vessels flying their flag or of their registry. Such laws and regulations shall at least have the same effect as that of generally accepted international rules and standards established through the competent international organization or general diplomatic conference.

3. States which establish particular requirements for the prevention, reduction and control of pollution of the marine environment as a condition for the entry of foreign vessels into their ports or internal waters or for a call at their off-shore terminals shall give due publicity to such requirements and shall communicate them to the competent international organization. Whenever such requirements are established in identical form by two or more coastal States in an endeavour to harmonize policy, the communication shall indicate which States are participating in such co-operative arrangements. Every State shall require the master of a vessel flying its flag or of its registry, when navigating within the territorial sea of a State participating in such co-operative arrangements, to furnish, upon the request of that State, information as to whether it is proceeding to a State of the same region participating in such co-operative arrangements and, if so, to indicate whether it complies with the port entry requirements of that State. This article is without prejudice to the continued exercise by a vessel of its right of innocent passage or to the application of article 25, paragraph 2.

4. Coastal States may, in the exercise of their sovereignty within their territorial sea, adopt laws and regulations for the prevention, reduction and control of marine pollution from foreign vessels, including vessels exercising the right of innocent passage. Such laws and regulations shall, in accordance with Part II, section 3, not hamper innocent passage of foreign vessels.

5. Coastal States, for the purpose of enforcement as provided for in section 6, may in respect of their exclusive economic zones adopt laws and regulations for the prevention, reduction and control of pollution from vessels conforming to and giving effect to generally accepted international rules and standards established through the competent international organization or general diplomatic conference.

6. (a) Where the international rules and standards referred to in paragraph 1 are inadequate to meet special circumstances and coastal States have reasonable grounds for believing that a particular, clearly defined area of their respective exclusive economic zones is an area where the adoption of special mandatory measures for the prevention of pollution from vessels is required for recognized technical reasons in relation to its oceanographical and ecological conditions, as well as its utilization or the protection of its resources and the particular character of its traffic, the coastal States, after appropriate consultations through the competent international organization with any other States concerned, may, for that area, direct a communication to that organization, submitting scientific and technical evidence in support and information on necessary reception facilities. Within 12 months after receiving such a communication, the organization shall determine whether the conditions in that area correspond to the requirements set out above. If the organization so determines, the coastal States may, for that area, adopt laws and regulations for the prevention, reduction and control of pollution from vessels implementing such international rules and standards or navigational practices as are made applicable, through the organization, for special areas. These laws and regulations shall not become applicable to foreign vessels until 15 months after the submission of the communication to the organization.

(b) The coastal States shall publish the limits of any such particular, clearly defined area.

(c) If the coastal States intend to adopt additional laws and regulations for the same area for the prevention, reduction and control of pollution from vessels, they shall, when submitting the aforesaid communication, at the same time notify the organization thereof. Such additional laws and regulations may relate to discharges or navigational practices but shall not require foreign vessels to observe design, construction, manning or equipment standards other than generally accepted international rules and standards; they shall become applicable to foreign vessels 15 months after the submission of the communication to the organization, provided that the organization agrees within 12 months after the submission of the communication.

7. The international rules and standards referred to in this article should include *inter alia* those relating to prompt notification to coastal States, whose coastline or related interests may be affected by incidents, including maritime casualties, which involve discharges or probability of discharges.

Article 212

Pollution from or through the atmosphere

1. States shall adopt laws and regulations to prevent, reduce and control pollution of the marine environment from or through the atmosphere, applicable to the air space under their sovereignty and to vessels flying their flag or vessels or aircraft of their registry, taking into account internationally agreed rules, standards and recommended practices and procedures and the safety of air navigation.

2. States shall take other measures as may be necessary to prevent, reduce and control such pollution.

3. States, acting especially through competent international organizations or diplomatic conference, shall endeavour to establish global and regional rules, standards and recommended practices and procedures to prevent, reduce and control such pollution.

SECTION 6. ENFORCEMENT

Article 213

Enforcement with respect to pollution from land-based sources

States shall enforce their laws and regulations adopted in accordance with article 207 and shall adopt laws and regulations and take other measures necessary to implement applicable international rules and standards established through competent international organizations or diplomatic conference to prevent, reduce and control pollution of the marine environment from land-based sources.

Article 214

Enforcement with respect to pollution from sea-bed activities

States shall enforce their laws and regulations adopted in accordance with article 208 and shall adopt laws and regulations and take other measures necessary to implement applicable international rules and standards established through competent international organizations or diplomatic conference to prevent, reduce and control pollution of the marine environment arising from or in connection with sea-bed activities subject to their jurisdiction and from artificial islands, installations and structures under their jurisdiction, pursuant to articles 60 and 80.

Article 215

Enforcement with respect to pollution from activities in the Area

Enforcement of international rules, regulations and procedures established in accordance with Part XI to prevent, reduce and control pollution of the marine environment from activities in the Area shall be governed by that Part.

Article 216

Enforcement with respect to pollution by dumping

1. Laws and regulations adopted in accordance with this Convention and applicable international rules and standards established through competent international organizations or diplomatic conference for the prevention, reduction and control of pollution of the marine environment by dumping shall be enforced:

(a) by the coastal State with regard to dumping within its territorial sea or its exclusive economic zone or onto its continental shelf;

(b) by the flag State with regard to vessels flying its flag or vessels or aircraft of its registry;

(c) by any State with regard to acts of loading of wastes or other matter occurring within its territory or at its off-shore terminals.

2. No State shall be obliged by virtue of this article to institute proceedings when another State has already instituted proceedings in accordance with this article.

Article 217

Enforcement by flag States

1. States shall ensure compliance by vessels flying their flag or of their registry with applicable international rules and standards, established through the competent international

organization or general diplomatic conference, and with their laws and regulations adopted in accordance with this Convention for the prevention, reduction and control of pollution of the marine environment from vessels and shall accordingly adopt laws and regulations and take other measures necessary for their implementation. Flag States shall provide for the effective enforcement of such rules, standards, laws and regulations, irrespective of where a violation occurs.

2. States shall, in particular, take appropriate measures in order to ensure that vessels flying their flag or of their registry are prohibited from sailing, until they can proceed to sea in compliance with the requirements of the international rules and standards referred to in paragraph 1, including requirements in respect of design, construction, equipment and manning of vessels.

3. States shall ensure that vessels flying their flag or of their registry carry on board certificates required by and issued pursuant to international rules and standards referred to in paragraph 1. States shall ensure that vessels flying their flag are periodically inspected in order to verify that such certificates are in conformity with the actual condition of the vessels. These certificates shall be accepted by other States as evidence of the condition of the vessels and shall be regarded as having the same force as certificates issued by them, unless there are clear grounds for believing that the condition of the vessel does not correspond substantially with the particulars of the certificates.

4. If a vessel commits a violation of rules and standards established through the competent international organization or general diplomatic conference, the flag State, without prejudice to articles 218, 220 and 228, shall provide for immediate investigation and where appropriate institute proceedings in respect of the alleged violation irrespective of where the violation occurred or where the pollution caused by such violation has occurred or has been spotted.

5. Flag States conducting an investigation of the violation may request the assistance of any other State whose co-operation could be useful in clarifying the circumstances of the case. States shall endeavour to meet appropriate requests of flag States.

6. States shall, at the written request of any State, investigate any violation alleged to have been committed by vessels flying their flag. If satisfied that sufficient evidence is available to enable proceedings to be brought in respect of the alleged violation, flag States shall without delay institute such proceedings in accordance with their laws.

7. Flag States shall promptly inform the requesting State and the competent international organization of the action taken and its outcome. Such information shall be available to all States.

8. Penalties provided for by the laws and regulations of States for vessels flying their flag shall be adequate in severity to discourage violations wherever they occur.

Article 218

Enforcement by port States

1. When a vessel is voluntarily within a port or at an off-shore terminal of a State, that State may undertake investigations and, where the evidence so warrants, institute proceedings in respect of any discharge from that vessel outside the internal waters, territorial sea or exclusive economic zone of that State in violation of applicable international rules and standards established through the competent international organization or general diplomatic conference.

2. No proceedings pursuant to paragraph 1 shall be instituted in respect of a discharge violation in the internal waters, territorial sea or exclusive economic zone of another State unless requested by that State, the flag State, or a State damaged or threatened by the discharge violation, or unless the violation has caused or is likely to cause pollution in the internal waters, territorial sea or exclusive economic zone of the State instituting the proceedings.

3. When a vessel is voluntarily within a port or at an off-shore terminal of a State, that State shall, as far as practicable, comply with requests from any State for investigation of a discharge violation referred to in paragraph 1, believed to have occurred in, caused, or threatened damage to the internal waters, territorial sea or exclusive economic zone of the requesting State. It shall likewise, as far as practicable, comply with requests from the flag State for investigation of such a violation, irrespective of where the violation occurred.

4. The records of the investigation carried out by a port State pursuant to this article shall be transmitted upon request to the flag State or to the coastal State. Any proceedings instituted by the port State on the basis of such an investigation may, subject to section 7, be suspended at the request of the coastal State when the violation has occurred within its internal waters, territorial sea or exclusive economic zone. The evidence and records of the case, together with any bond or other financial security posted with the authorities of the port State, shall in that event be transmitted to the coastal State. Such transmittal shall preclude the continuation of proceedings in the port State.

Article 219

Measures relating to seaworthiness of vessels to avoid pollution

Subject to section 7, States which, upon request or on their own initiative, have ascertained that a vessel within one of their ports or at one of their off-shore terminals is in violation of applicable international rules and standards relating to seaworthiness of vessels and thereby threatens damage to the marine environment shall, as far as practicable, take administrative measures to prevent the vessel from sailing. Such States may permit the vessel to proceed only to the nearest appropriate repair yard and, upon removal of the causes of the violation, shall permit the vessel to continue immediately.

Article 220

Enforcement by coastal States

1. When a vessel is voluntarily within a port or at an off-shore terminal of a State, that State may, subject to section 7, institute proceedings in respect of any violation of its laws and regulations adopted in accordance with this Convention or applicable international rules and standards for the prevention, reduction and control of pollution from vessels when the violation has occurred within the territorial sea or the exclusive economic zone of that State.

2. Where there are clear grounds for believing that a vessel navigating in the territorial sea of a State has, during its passage therein, violated laws and regulations of that State adopted in accordance with this Convention or applicable international rules and standards for the prevention, reduction and control of pollution from vessels, that State, without prejudice to the application of the relevant provisions of Part II, section 3, may undertake physical inspection of the vessel relating to the violation and may, where the evidence so warrants,

institute proceedings, including detention of the vessel, in accordance with its laws, subject to the provisions of section 7.

3. Where there are clear grounds for believing that a vessel navigating in the exclusive economic zone or the territorial sea of a State has, in the exclusive economic zone, committed a violation of applicable international rules and standards for the prevention, reduction and control of pollution from vessels or laws and regulations of that State conforming and giving effect to such rules and standards, that State may require the vessel to give information regarding its identity and port of registry, its last and its next port of call and other relevant information required to establish whether a violation has occurred.

4. States shall adopt laws and regulations and take other measures so that vessels flying their flag comply with requests for information pursuant to paragraph 3.

5. Where there are clear grounds for believing that a vessel navigating in the exclusive economic zone or the territorial sea of a State has, in the exclusive economic zone, committed a violation referred to in paragraph 3 resulting in a substantial discharge causing or threatening significant pollution of the marine environment, that State may undertake physical inspection of the vessel for matters relating to the violation if the vessel has refused to give information or if the information supplied by the vessel is manifestly at variance with the evident factual situation and if the circumstances of the case justify such inspection.

6. Where there is clear objective evidence that a vessel navigating in the exclusive economic zone or the territorial sea of a State has, in the exclusive economic zone, committed a violation referred to in paragraph 3 resulting in a discharge causing major damage or threat of major damage to the coastline or related interests of the coastal State, or to any resources of its territorial sea or exclusive economic zone, that State may, subject to section 7, provided that the evidence so warrants, institute proceedings, including detention of the vessel, in accordance with its laws.

7. Notwithstanding the provisions of paragraph 6, whenever appropriate procedures have been established, either through the competent international organization or as otherwise agreed, whereby compliance with requirements for bonding or other appropriate financial security has been assured, the coastal State if bound by such procedures shall allow the vessel to proceed.

8. The provisions of paragraphs 3, 4, 5, 6 and 7 also apply in respect of national laws and regulations adopted pursuant to article 211, paragraph 6.

Article 221

Measures to avoid pollution arising from maritime casualties

1. Nothing in this Part shall prejudice the right of States, pursuant to international law, both customary and conventional, to take and enforce measures beyond the territorial sea proportionate to the actual or threatened damage to protect their coastline or related interests, including fishing, from pollution or threat of pollution following upon a maritime casualty or acts relating to such a casualty, which may reasonably be expected to result in major harmful consequences.

2. For the purposes of this article, "maritime casualty" means a collision of vessels, stranding or other incident of navigation, or other occurrence on board a vessel or external to it resulting in material damage or imminent threat of material damage to a vessel or cargo.

Article 222

Enforcement with respect to pollution from or through the atmosphere
States shall enforce, within the air space under their sovereignty or with regard to vessels flying their flag or vessels or aircraft of their registry, their laws and regulations adopted in accordance with article 212, paragraph 1, and with other provisions of this Convention and shall adopt laws and regulations and take other measures necessary to implement applicable international rules and standards established through competent international organizations or diplomatic conference to prevent, reduce and control pollution of the marine environment from or through the atmosphere, in conformity with all relevant international rules and standards concerning the safety of air navigation.

• • •

Article 226

Investigation of foreign vessels
1. (a) States shall not delay a foreign vessel longer than is essential for purposes of the investigations provided for in articles 216, 218 and 220. Any physical inspection of a foreign vessel shall be limited to an examination of such certificates, records or other documents as the vessel is required to carry by generally accepted international rules and standards or of any similar documents which it is carrying; further physical inspection of the vessel may be undertaken only after such an examination and only when:
    (i) there are clear grounds for believing that the condition of the vessel or its equipment does not correspond substantially with the particulars of those documents;
    (ii) the contents of such documents are not sufficient to confirm or verify a suspected violation; or
    (iii) the vessel is not carrying valid certificates and records.
    (b) If the investigation indicates a violation of applicable laws and regulations or international rules and standards for the protection and preservation of the marine environment, release shall be made promptly subject to reasonable procedures such as bonding or other appropriate financial security.
    (c) Without prejudice to applicable international rules and standards relating to the seaworthiness of vessels, the release of a vessel may, whenever it would present an unreasonable threat of damage to the marine environment, be refused or made conditional upon proceeding to the nearest appropriate repair yard. Where release has been refused or made conditional, the flag State of the vessel must be promptly notified, and may seek release of the vessel in accordance with Part XV.
2. States shall co-operate to develop procedures for the avoidance of unnecessary physical inspection of vessels at sea.

• • •

Article 228

Suspension and restrictions on institution of proceedings
1. Proceedings to impose penalties in respect of any violation of applicable laws and regulations or international rules and standards relating to the prevention, reduction and control of pollution from vessels committed by a foreign vessel beyond the territorial sea of

the State instituting proceedings shall be suspended upon the taking of proceedings to impose penalties in respect of corresponding charges by the flag State within six months of the date on which proceedings were first instituted, unless those proceedings relate to a case of major damage to the coastal State or the flag State in question has repeatedly disregarded its obligations to enforce effectively the applicable international rules and standards in respect of violations committed by its vessels. The flag State shall in due course make available to the State previously instituting proceedings a full dossier of the case and the records of the proceedings, whenever the flag State has requested the suspension of proceedings in accordance with this article. When proceedings instituted by the flag State have been brought to a conclusion, the suspended proceedings shall be terminated. Upon payment of costs incurred in respect of such proceedings, any bond posted or other financial security provided in connection with the suspended proceedings shall be released by the coastal State.

2. Proceedings to impose penalties on foreign vessels shall not be instituted after the expiry of three years from the date on which the violation was committed, and shall not be taken by any State in the event of proceedings having been instituted by another State subject to the provisions set out in paragraph 1.

3. The provisions of this article are without prejudice to the right of the flag State to take any measures, including proceedings to impose penalties, according to its laws irrespective of prior proceedings by another State.

• • •

SECTION 8. ICE-COVERED AREAS

Article 234

Ice-covered areas

Coastal States have the right to adopt and enforce non-discriminatory laws and regulations for the prevention, reduction and control of marine pollution from vessels in ice-covered areas within the limits of the exclusive economic zone, where particularly severe climatic conditions and the presence of ice covering such areas for most of the year create obstructions or exceptional hazards to navigation, and pollution of the marine environment could cause major harm to or irreversible disturbance of the ecological balance. Such laws and regulations shall have due regard to navigation and the protection and preservation of the marine environment based on the best available scientific evidence.

SECTION 9. RESPONSIBILITY AND LIABILITY

Article 235

Responsibility and liability

1. States are responsible for the fulfilment of their international obligations concerning the protection and preservation of the marine environment. They shall be liable in accordance with international law.

2. States shall ensure that recourse is available in accordance with their legal systems for prompt and adequate compensation or other relief in respect of damage caused by pollution of the marine environment by natural or juridical persons under their jurisdiction.

148 International Law — Documentary Supplement

3. With the objective of assuring prompt and adequate compensation in respect of all damage caused by pollution of the marine environment, States shall co-operate in the implementation of existing international law and the further development of international law relating to responsibility and liability for the assessment of and compensation for damage and the settlement of related disputes, as well as, where appropriate, development of criteria and procedures for payment of adequate compensation, such as compulsory insurance or compensation funds.

• • •

PART XV
SETTLEMENT OF DISPUTES

SECTION 1. GENERAL PROVISIONS

Article 279

Obligation to settle disputes by peaceful means

States Parties shall settle any dispute between them concerning the interpretation or application of this Convention by peaceful means in accordance with Article 2, paragraph 3, of the Charter of the United Nations and, to this end, shall seek a solution by the means indicated in Article 33, paragraph 1, of the Charter.

Article 280

Settlement of disputes by any peaceful means chosen by the parties

Nothing in this Part impairs the right of any States Parties to agree at any time to settle a dispute between them concerning the interpretation or application of this Convention by any peaceful means of their own choice.

Article 281

Procedure where no settlement has been reached by the parties

1. If the States Parties which are parties to a dispute concerning the interpretation or application of this Convention have agreed to seek settlement of the dispute by a peaceful means of their own choice, the procedures provided for in this Part apply only where no settlement has been reached by recourse to such means and the agreement between the parties does not exclude any further procedure.

2. If the parties have also agreed on a time-limit, paragraph 1 applies only upon the expiration of that time-limit.

Article 282

Obligations under general, regional or bilateral agreements

If the States Parties which are parties to a dispute concerning the interpretation or application of this Convention have agreed, through a general, regional or bilateral agreement or otherwise, that such dispute shall, at the request of any party to the dispute, be submitted to a procedure that entails a binding decision, that procedure shall apply in lieu of the procedures provided for in this Part, unless the parties to the dispute otherwise agree.

Article 283

Obligation to exchange views

1. When a dispute arises between States Parties concerning the interpretation or application of this Convention, the parties to the dispute shall proceed expeditiously to an exchange of views regarding its settlement by negotiation or other peaceful means.

2. The parties shall also proceed expeditiously to an exchange of views where a procedure for the settlement of such a dispute has been terminated without a settlement or where a settlement has been reached and the circumstances require consultation regarding the manner of implementing the settlement.

Article 284

Conciliation

1. A State Party which is a party to a dispute concerning the interpretation or application of this Convention may invite the other party or parties to submit the dispute to conciliation in accordance with the procedure under Annex V, section 1, or another conciliation procedure.

2. If the invitation is accepted and if the parties agree upon the conciliation procedure to be applied, any party may submit the dispute to that procedure.

3. If the invitation is not accepted or the parties do not agree upon the procedure, the conciliation proceedings shall be deemed to be terminated.

4. Unless the parties otherwise agree, when a dispute has been submitted to conciliation, the proceedings may be terminated only in accordance with the agreed conciliation procedure.

Article 285

Application of this section to disputes submitted pursuant to Part XI

This section applies to any dispute which pursuant to Part XI, section 5, is to be settled in accordance with procedures provided for in this Part. If an entity other than a State Party is a party to such a dispute, this section applies mutatis mutandis.

SECTION 2. COMPULSORY PROCEDURES ENTAILING BINDING DECISIONS

Article 286

Application of procedures under this section

Subject to section 3, any dispute concerning the interpretation or application of this Convention shall, where no settlement has been reached by recourse to section 1, be submitted at the request of any party to the dispute to the court or tribunal having jurisdiction under this section.

Article 287

Choice of procedure

1. When signing, ratifying or acceding to this Convention or at any time thereafter, a State shall be free to choose, by means of a written declaration, one or more of the following means for the settlement of disputes concerning the interpretation or application of this Convention:

(a) the International Tribunal for the Law of the Sea established in accordance with Annex VI;

(b) the International Court of Justice;

(c) an arbitral tribunal constituted in accordance with Annex VII;

(d) a special arbitral tribunal constituted in accordance with Annex VIII for one or more of the categories of disputes specified therein.

2. A declaration made under paragraph 1 shall not affect or be affected by the obligation of a State Party to accept the jurisdiction of the Seabed Disputes Chamber of the International Tribunal for the Law of the Sea to the extent and in the manner provided for in Part XI, section 5.

3. A State Party, which is a party to a dispute not covered by a declaration in force, shall be deemed to have accepted arbitration in accordance with Annex VII.

4. If the parties to a dispute have accepted the same procedure for the settlement of the dispute, it may be submitted only to that procedure, unless the parties otherwise agree.

5. If the parties to a dispute have not accepted the same procedure for the settlement of the dispute, it may be submitted only to arbitration in accordance with Annex VII, unless the parties otherwise agree.

6. A declaration made under paragraph 1 shall remain in force until three months after notice of revocation has been deposited with the Secretary-General of the United Nations.

7. A new declaration, a notice of revocation or the expiry of a declaration does not in any way affect proceedings pending before a court or tribunal having jurisdiction under this article, unless the parties otherwise agree.

8. Declarations and notices referred to in this article shall be deposited with the Secretary-General of the United Nations, who shall transmit copies thereof to the States Parties.

Article 288

Jurisdiction

1. A court or tribunal referred to in article 287 shall have jurisdiction over any dispute concerning the interpretation or application of this Convention which is submitted to it in accordance with this Part.

2. A court or tribunal referred to in article 287 shall also have jurisdiction over any dispute concerning the interpretation or application of an international agreement related to the purposes of this Convention, which is submitted to it in accordance with the agreement.

3. The Seabed Disputes Chamber of the International Tribunal for the Law of the Sea established in accordance with Annex VI, and any other chamber or arbitral tribunal referred to in Part XI, section 5, shall have jurisdiction in any matter which is submitted to it in accordance therewith.

4. In the event of a dispute as to whether a court or tribunal has jurisdiction, the matter shall be settled by decision of that court or tribunal.

Article 289

Experts

In any dispute involving scientific or technical matters, a court or tribunal exercising jurisdiction under this section may, at the request of a party or proprio motu, select in consultation with the parties no fewer than two scientific or technical experts chosen preferably from the relevant list prepared in accordance with Annex VIII, article 2, to sit with the court or tribunal but without the right to vote.

Article 290

Provisional measures

1. If a dispute has been duly submitted to a court or tribunal which considers that prima facie it has jurisdiction under this Part or Part XI, section 5, the court or tribunal may prescribe any provisional measures which it considers appropriate under the circumstances to preserve the respective rights of the parties to the dispute or to prevent serious harm to the marine environment, pending the final decision.

2. Provisional measures may be modified or revoked as soon as the circumstances justifying them have changed or ceased to exist.

3. Provisional measures may be prescribed, modified or revoked under this article only at the request of a party to the dispute and after the parties have been given an opportunity to be heard.

4. The court or tribunal shall forthwith give notice to the parties to the dispute, and to such other States Parties as it considers appropriate, of the prescription, modification or revocation of provisional measures.

5. Pending the constitution of an arbitral tribunal to which a dispute is being submitted under this section, any court or tribunal agreed upon by the parties or, failing such agreement within two weeks from the date of the request for provisional measures, the International Tribunal for the Law of the Sea or, with respect to activities in the Area, the Seabed Disputes Chamber, may prescribe, modify or revoke provisional measures in accordance with this article if it considers that prima facie the tribunal which is to be constituted would have jurisdiction and that the urgency of the situation so requires. Once constituted, the tribunal to which the dispute has been submitted may modify, revoke or affirm those provisional measures, acting in conformity with paragraphs 1 to 4.

6. The parties to the dispute shall comply promptly with any provisional measures prescribed under this article.

Article 291

Access

1. All the dispute settlement procedures specified in this Part shall be open to States Parties.

2. The dispute settlement procedures specified in this Part shall be open to entities other than States Parties only as specifically provided for in this Convention.

Article 292

Prompt release of vessels and crews

1. Where the authorities of a State Party have detained a vessel flying the flag of another State Party and it is alleged that the detaining State has not complied with the provisions of this Convention for the prompt release of the vessel or its crew upon the posting of a reasonable bond or other financial security, the question of release from detention may be submitted to any court or tribunal agreed upon by the parties or, failing such agreement within 10 days from the time of detention, to a court or tribunal accepted by the detaining State under article 287 or to the International Tribunal for the Law of the Sea, unless the parties otherwise agree.

2. The application for release may be made only by or on behalf of the flag State of the vessel.

3. The court or tribunal shall deal without delay with the application for release and shall deal only with the question of release, without prejudice to the merits of any case before the appropriate domestic forum against the vessel, its owner or its crew. The authorities of the detaining State remain competent to release the vessel or its crew at any time.

4. Upon the posting of the bond or other financial security determined by the court or tribunal, the authorities of the detaining State shall comply promptly with the decision of the court or tribunal concerning the release of the vessel or its crew.

Article 293

Applicable law

1. A court or tribunal having jurisdiction under this section shall apply this Convention and other rules of international law not incompatible with this Convention.

2. Paragraph 1 does not prejudice the power of the court or tribunal having jurisdiction under this section to decide a case ex aequo et bono, if the parties so agree.

Article 294

Preliminary proceedings

1. A court or tribunal provided for in article 287 to which an application is made in respect of a dispute referred to in article 297 shall determine at the request of a party, or may determine proprio motu, whether the claim constitutes an abuse of legal process or whether prima facie it is well founded. If the court or tribunal determines that the claim constitutes an abuse of legal process or is prima facie unfounded, it shall take no further action in the case.

2. Upon receipt of the application, the court or tribunal shall immediately notify the other party or parties of the application, and shall fix a reasonable time-limit within which they may request it to make a determination in accordance with paragraph 1.

3. Nothing in this article affects the right of any party to a dispute to make preliminary objections in accordance with the applicable rules of procedure.

Article 295

Exhaustion of local remedies

Any dispute between States Parties concerning the interpretation or application of this Convention may be submitted to the procedures provided for in this section only after local remedies have been exhausted where this is required by international law.

Article 296

Finality and binding force of decisions

1. Any decision rendered by a court or tribunal having jurisdiction under this section shall be final and shall be complied with by all the parties to the dispute.

2. Any such decision shall have no binding force except between the parties and in respect of that particular dispute.

SECTION 3. LIMITATIONS AND EXCEPTIONS TO APPLICABILITY OF SECTION 2

Article 297

Limitations on applicability of section 2

1. Disputes concerning the interpretation or application of this Convention with regard to the exercise by a coastal State of its sovereign rights or jurisdiction provided for in this Convention shall be subject to the procedures provided for in section 2 in the following cases:

(a) when it is alleged that a coastal State has acted in contravention of the provisions of this Convention in regard to the freedoms and rights of navigation, overflight or the laying of submarine cables and pipelines, or in regard to other internationally lawful uses of the sea specified in article 58;

(b) when it is alleged that a State in exercising the aforementioned freedoms, rights or uses has acted in contravention of this Convention or of laws or regulations adopted by the coastal State in conformity with this Convention and other rules of international law not incompatible with this Convention; or

(c) when it is alleged that a coastal State has acted in contravention of specified international rules and standards for the protection and preservation of the marine environment which are applicable to the coastal State and which have been established by this Convention or through a competent international organization or diplomatic conference in accordance with this Convention.

2. (a) Disputes concerning the interpretation or application of the provisions of this Convention with regard to marine scientific research shall be settled in accordance with section 2, except that the coastal State shall not be obliged to accept the submission to such settlement of any dispute arising out of:

(i) the exercise by the coastal State of a right or discretion in accordance with article 246; or

(ii) a decision by the coastal State to order suspension or cessation of a research project in accordance with article 253.

(b) A dispute arising from an allegation by the researching State that with respect to a specific project the coastal State is not exercising its rights under articles 246 and 253 in a manner compatible with this Convention shall be submitted, at the request of either party, to conciliation under Annex V, section 2, provided that the conciliation commission shall not call in question the exercise by the coastal State of its discretion to designate specific areas as referred to in article 246, paragraph 6, or of its discretion to withhold consent in accordance with article 246, paragraph 5.

3. (a) Disputes concerning the interpretation or application of the provisions of this Convention with regard to fisheries shall be settled in accordance with section 2, except that the coastal State shall not be obliged to accept the submission to such settlement of any dispute relating to its sovereign rights with respect to the living resources in the exclusive economic zone or their exercise, including its discretionary powers for determining the allowable catch, its harvesting capacity, the allocation of surpluses to other States and the terms and conditions established in its conservation and management laws and regulations.

(b) Where no settlement has been reached by recourse to section 1 of this Part, a dispute shall be submitted to conciliation under Annex V, section 2, at the request of any party to the dispute, when it is alleged that:

(i) a coastal State has manifestly failed to comply with its obligations to ensure through proper conservation and management measures that the maintenance of the living resources in the exclusive economic zone is not seriously endangered;

(ii) a coastal State has arbitrarily refused to determine, at the request of another State, the allowable catch and its capacity to harvest living resources with respect to stocks which that other State is interested in fishing; or

(iii) a coastal State has arbitrarily refused to allocate to any State, under articles 62, 69 and 70 and under the terms and conditions established by the coastal State consistent with this Convention, the whole or part of the surplus it has declared to exist.

(c) In no case shall the conciliation commission substitute its discretion for that of the coastal State.

(d) The report of the conciliation commission shall be communicated to the appropriate international organizations.

(e) In negotiating agreements pursuant to articles 69 and 70, States Parties, unless they otherwise agree, shall include a clause on measures which they shall take in order to minimize the possibility of a disagreement concerning the interpretation or application of the agreement, and on how they should proceed if a disagreement nevertheless arises.

Article 298

Optional exceptions to applicability of section 2

1. When signing, ratifying or acceding to this Convention or at any time thereafter, a State may, without prejudice to the obligations arising under section 1, declare in writing that it does not accept any one or more of the procedures provided for in section 2 with respect to one or more of the following categories of disputes:

(a) (i) disputes concerning the interpretation or application of articles 15, 74 and 83 relating to sea boundary delimitations, or those involving historic bays or titles, provided that a State having made such a declaration shall, when such a dispute arises subsequent to the entry into force of this Convention and where no agreement within a reasonable period of time is reached in negotiations between the parties, at the request of any party to the dispute, accept submission of the matter to conciliation under Annex V, section 2; and provided further that any dispute that necessarily involves the concurrent consideration of any unsettled dispute concerning sovereignty or other rights over continental or insular land territory shall be excluded from such submission;

(ii) after the conciliation commission has presented its report, which shall state the reasons on which it is based, the parties shall negotiate an agreement on the basis of that report; if these negotiations do not result in an agreement, the parties shall, by mutual consent, submit the question to one of the procedures provided for in section 2, unless the parties otherwise agree;

(iii) this subparagraph does not apply to any sea boundary dispute finally settled by an arrangement between the parties, or to any such dispute which is to be settled in accordance with a bilateral or multilateral agreement binding upon those parties;

(b) disputes concerning military activities, including military activities by government vessels and aircraft engaged in non-commercial service, and disputes concerning law enforcement activities in regard to the exercise of sovereign rights or jurisdiction excluded from the jurisdiction of a court or tribunal under article 297, paragraph 2 or 3;

(c) disputes in respect of which the Security Council of the United Nations is exercising the functions assigned to it by the Charter of the United Nations, unless the Security Council decides to remove the matter from its agenda or calls upon the parties to settle it by the means provided for in this Convention.

2. A State Party which has made a declaration under paragraph 1 may at any time withdraw it, or agree to submit a dispute excluded by such declaration to any procedure specified in this Convention.

3. A State Party which has made a declaration under paragraph 1 shall not be entitled to submit any dispute falling within the excepted category of disputes to any procedure in this Convention as against another State Party, without the consent of that party.

4. If one of the States Parties has made a declaration under paragraph 1(a), any other State Party may submit any dispute falling within an excepted category against the declarant party to the procedure specified in such declaration.

5. A new declaration, or the withdrawal of a declaration, does not in any way affect proceedings pending before a court or tribunal in accordance with this article, unless the parties otherwise agree.

6. Declarations and notices of withdrawal of declarations under this article shall be deposited with the Secretary-General of the United Nations, who shall transmit copies thereof to the States Parties.

Article 299

Right of the parties to agree upon a procedure

1. A dispute excluded under article 297 or excepted by a declaration made under article 298 from the dispute settlement procedures provided for in section 2 may be submitted to such procedures only by agreement of the parties to the dispute.

2. Nothing in this section impairs the right of the parties to the dispute to agree to some other procedure for the settlement of such dispute or to reach an amicable settlement.

• • •

PART XVII
FINAL PROVISIONS

Article 309

Reservations and exceptions

No reservations or exceptions may be made to this Convention unless expressly permitted by other articles of this Convention.